MW00579615

WHAT IS TRUE LOVE? ACCORDING TO THE BIBLE

PLEASE NOTE: What is True Love? According to the Bible has come about after a couple of decades of Bible study and introspection. Various pastors, priests, and ministers have been consulted and every single one vehemently disagrees with my findings. I have been excommunicated by the Catholic Church and am now officially a heretic.

The above credentials are the best that I can come up with.

Another Sola Scriptura publication from Mosaic House Co.

Various public domain Bible translations such as the King James and Literal Translation have been utilised for the Scripture quoted in 'How To Love According to God's Will.' We thank the Bible translators who made GOD's Word freely available to us all through the public domain. For my research, I use multiple other resources including Jewish Bible, JPS Hebrew-English, Strong's Exhaustive Concordance of the Bible, The Brown-Driver-Briggs Hebrew and Eglish Lexikon and more as can be found on this link, which lists some of my favourite Biblical resources,

https://liveforeverhowto.wordpress.com/2016/05/06/15-of-my-best-and-favourite-biblical-resources

All Scriptural references are provided so that readers can do their own research using their preferred Bible translation. To get the message across succinctly for readers who are not familiar with the Bible, occasionally I've paraphrased Scripture 'the Aussie way.' This may not be politically correct but is done to improve the readability of this study.

For the full story download a free Bible.

Mosaic House Co., Post box 25 Noosa, Queensland 4567, Australia

Or visit us at http://mosaichouse.co/

ISBN: 978-1-925944-09-9
With special thanks to Red Hat Inc.
Made in the Commonwealth of Australia.
Published in the United States of America
Cover design by M Emmanuel
Layout and formatting by SunnyEdesign
Editor Elaine Roughton
written in 2009 and published in 2019 – ©myemmanuel

A SPECIAL NOTE for my friends who believe differently: I love you.

LOVE EACH OTHER. KEEP HIS COMMANDMENTS. JUDGE NOT.
THE LORD IS OUR JUDGE AND LAWGIVER. WATCH OUT!

By this shall all men know that ye are my disciples, if ye have love one to another. John 13:35 By this we know that we love the children of God, when we love God, and keep his commandments. 1 John 5:2 *John answered him, saying, Master, we saw one casting out devils in your name, and he doesn't follow us: and we forbade him, because he does not follow us. But Jesus said, Forbid him not: for there is no man which shall do a miracle in my name, that can lightly speak evil of me. Mark 9:38-39* Judge not, that ye be not judged. For with what judgment ye judge, ye shall be judged: and with what measure ye mete, it shall be measured to you again. Matthew 7:1-2 *For the Lord is our judge, the Lord is our lawgiver, the Lord is our king; he will save us. Isaiah 33:22* To the law and to the testimony: if they speak not according to this word, it is because there is no light in them. Isaiah 8:20 *Jesus said, Be careful, watch out for the deceit of the Pharisees and of the Sadducees. Matthew 16:6*

CONTENTS

What is True Love According to the Bible?
Reviews from Amazon customers

5 stars **A well written manual about true love based on the Bible!**
I loved this book. The author shares her reflections and research based on in depth study of Scriptures. She writes in clear concise terms and dispels the myths about true love — being just unconditional!
I appreciated the stories and action steps enlisted in this book to understand and practice what true love really means. I highly recommend this read. It's interesting, thought provoking and different. I will come back to this book again to study in depth the references cited. Anita Oommen, bestselling author of *Picking Up The Shards.*

5 stars **Great read!** *What i love about this book is that the author shares so many example on how love is used in her life (based on the bible scriptures). Its easy read with lots of insight but more importantly lots of deep provoking questions to help you reflect on life. Highly recommend this book.* PetrosE

5 stars **A Very Good Look at True Love** *A lot of people claim to be in love or are in relationships, but aren't really happy. This books does a good job at explaining what true and lasting love is (And is not) and how to take action to have it and create it in your own life. It's an easy read, but has a lot to think about and apply in your life.* Melanie

5 stars **Excellent read.** *Excellent read that helps frame and put into perspective Love and what true love is. I really enjoyed reading this!* JB

DEDICATION

*Remember my words in your heart and soul…
and teach them to your children
(Deuteronomy 11:18-21)*

This book is written for my daughters, my Godson, and their peers because we're told to teach our children about God's Word.

How to apply God's Word to our daily lives? By finding out what true love is according to the Bible.

What on earth could be more important to learn about than 'How to love?'

Next: Many Thanks

MANY THANKS

I acknowledge the contributions of the prophetesses Huldah, Sarah, Miriam, Deborah, Hannah, Abigail, Esther, and Anna, as mentioned in the Bible, and Catherine Booth, from Ashbourne, Derbyshire in England, also known as, 'The Mother' of the Salvation Army. I thank them for being such wonderful role models.

Thank you to my Mum for giving me a daily dose of 'Jesus stories' when I was little. I treasure those times.

Thank you to all my proof and beta readers for your invaluable feedback. Many thanks to my faithful editor Elaine and formatter Jenny and my invaluable assistant Sunny.

Many thanks also to the wonderful team and support workers at Centacare who support me in many different ways whilst I write my books. I love you all!

Next: Who Am I?

Who Am I

My name is Mimi Emmanuel and you may wonder what my qualifications are for writing about 'True Love According To The Bible' and such glorious subjects as 'This is Love According To God's Will.'

I'm a student of God's Holy Word and the author of 'God Healed me' which became an international bestseller and has been in the top one hundred bestselling books on Amazon in the categories of, 'Religious Studies,' 'Prayer books,' and 'Adult Christian Ministry' since publication in May 2016.

You can find out more about me and my credentials on my blog www.liveforeverhowto.wordpress.com under 'Qualifications' and the 'Please don't get me into trouble' post.

Next: Foreword

FOREWORD

"It has been such a joy and delight to see Mimi's heart on paper.

This book looks at the fundamental components Jesus not only taught, but modelled Himself.

It explores the practicality of love and identifies the cost involved in truly loving others the way Jesus does.

Mimi writes in a way that shows the every day human being how we in the 21st century can actively apply the words of Jesus today, how we can challenge our egocentric culture and how we can positively influence the world around us.

I admire her rawness in sharing her own personal experiences around her spiritual growth.

She beautifully touches on the highs and the lows of doing her Christian life with people.

Despite the hurt from previous relationships in and out of church, she actively seeks to live a proactive life of gentleness, faithfulness, forgiveness and above all, love.

A great read for the seeker and the believer."

Naomi Oksanen – Pastor of C3 Limitless Church

Next: Introduction

INTRODUCTION

Anyone who doesn't love
does not know God,
because God is love.
(1 John 4:8)

I'm no expert on love. I failed too many times to call myself an expert. What my failings inspired me to do, however, is to learn about love. I became desperate to find out what true love is.

Not the kind of love where people are together out of convenience or to raise the kids, or because he or she can elevate one's status, or a million other reasons. I yearned to find out about true love.

I've experienced what I call 'true love' from my Mum, and from other family members. But am I measuring up?

Love others as yourself
Love others as you love yourself...
(Leviticus 19:18, Matthew 19:19)

In the past I certainly was not truly loving myself, that's for sure. If I had sufficient love for myself, I would never have allowed my health to crumble as it did.

15

It's hard, if not impossible, to be truly loving others if you aren't giving yourself that same respect.

My search for a template

Some of my relationships didn't go as well as they could have, for the reasons mentioned and also because there were no guidelines, no rules other than 'anything goes.'

'I won't criticise you, if you leave me alone.'

'I'm just experimenting, what's wrong with you? Can't you take a joke? You're so sensitive!'

'What's it to you what I do? Let me be!'

I CRAVED rules. I CRAVED guidelines and a 'normal.' I desperately needed and sought guidance to be a good Mum and wife. To be truly loving without losing my integrity.

I needed a template for living and loving. I searched for it high and low because the turmoil and disruptions of 'anything goes,' didn't work for me.

I struggled to raise babies and little children in an environment where rules were made up from moment to moment and anyone did whatever was right in their own eyes.

When I was little I treasured the 'Jesus stories' that my Mum read out to me. I didn't realise until I was well into my forties that these were TRUE stories and parables told by the greatest teacher of all times.

When I embraced Jesus as the true love of my life I finally learned how to love truly. Yes, I've fallen head over heels and am supremely grateful for the lessons and ongoing tuition that I'm receiving.

Whilst before I groped in the dark, now I'm basking in the light and love from the Father and His Son.

I can think of no better source to find out about true love than from Jesus and His Father.

I set out to find out what does 'loving the Christian way' mean? Is it different from 'mainstream' loving?

Salvation

We're told that the Central Message of the Bible is one of salvation. Sure, I reckon the Holy Word spells out quite succinctly how to save us from ourselves. And I say this only partially tongue in cheek.

What if the salvation story, you know, the faith and grace, is just part of the story? What if the main premise is one of love? A life filled with love now. Not later. Not once you've died and gone to heaven; if you would be so lucky. But right now!

Love truly
This small book is about how to love truly according to The Bible. I'll be quoting what our Father and His Son say about it.

I love Marie Kondo, the decluttering expert. Her motto is that we should 'get rid of things that don't spark joy in our lives.'

You can consider this book like a 'Marie Kondo' shortcut on 'how-to-love-truly.'

Ancient wisdom
it's not my own words I speak. I merely repeat age-old-wisdom which has been ignored, forgotten, and misinterpreted for millennia.

I pray this to be a wake-up call for the reader as it was a wake-up call for me when I came across this ancient text.

Next: Researching True Love

RESEARCHING TRUE LOVE

Do We Have a Universal Love Language?

People quote from the Bible all the time. But I hardly ever hear people correctly quote what our Father and His Son say about true love.

Every Christian I meet tells me how much Jesus and His Father love me. I rarely hear anyone mention that love is always a two-way street. There is no true love without that exchange. Just as there is a limit to a mother's unconditional love,' and I speak from experience.

If you're basking in that 'unconditional love' that's forever flowing from heaven, this book will challenge you and those ideas.

Whilst doing research for this book, I randomly asked various people, 'What is true love?'

Some music fans referred to Pink's hit single 'True Love,' which starts off saying that sometimes she 'hates every single stupid word that he says.'

That's not my kinda love.

Others mentioned a song by Tex Perkins where he sings that *'Love is doing the dishes.'* And I remember the signature tune of the 'Minder' series, *'I could be so good for you,'* sung by Dennis Waterman.

These are sentiments that I agree with.

Most people I asked about true love agreed that it involves mutual respect, trust, honesty, acceptance, loyalty, empathy, and commitment.

When I asked people specifically, 'What is love according to the Bible?'

Many answered something like, 'We are to love others as ourselves', or, 'We are to love our neighbour as ourselves.' Some people said that 'God is love,' and 'love is kind and patient and so on,' or, 'we must obey.'

And whilst all of this is true, these are summations and hardly tell us 'how to love' and what 'true love' is.

Do unto others
If, for instance, we were to just say, 'greet others the way you would like to be greeted,' you could get in serious trouble.

Tibetans greet by poking out the tongue, Japanese people bow to each other, some African tribes jump as high as they can during meetings, while many European cultures kiss and shake hands. The variations are endless.

Telling someone to love or greet others the way you like to be loved or greeted may work if you have learned how to love and care for yourself and whilst you move around in your own neighbourhood. But as soon as you travel and meet with people from other cultures, you'll need a universal language that is safe and works in each and every situation.

Love language
Does such a (love) language exist?

Yes it does. God's Holy Word elaborates on how to 'love others as ourselves' and tells us in great detail what true, fearless love is, and how we are to reciprocate.

There is no fear in love
There is no fear in love
True love for others is fearless.
If the thought of repercussions scares us,
this means that we have not
really learned to love.
(1 John 4:18)

If you experience fear in your relationships you have not learned how to truly love.

Remember how earlier it was mentioned that we have to learn to love ourselves first?

Love your neighbour as yourself
Love your neighbour as yourself…
(Leviticus 19:18, Matthew 19:19)

Love others as yourself. You need to love yourself first and take care of yourself before you can love others fearlessly.

Are you keeping yourself safe from harm?

Do you experience fear of rejection, fear of abandonment, fear of punishment, fear of not being loved back equally? This is a BIG one. We all want to be loved. But are we fearful of not being good enough to be loved? Are we loving *ourselves* as well as *others* fearlessly?

Next: How To Read This Book

How to Read this Book

According to Guinness World Records, the Bible is the best-selling book of all time, with an estimated 5 billion copies sold and distributed.

The Bible has been translated into many languages from the Biblical languages of Hebrew, Aramaic, and Greek. The full Bible has been translated into 670 languages, the New Testament has been translated into 1,521 languages, and Bible portions or stories into 1,121 other languages.

The Bible is and always has been the most popular book in the world. It was one of the first major mass-produced books printed by the Gutenberg printing press. Johannes Gutenberg invented the printing press in order to spread the Holy Bible in a more efficient manner.

Please have an open mind when you read this book. See if you can suspend judgment and lay preconceived ideas aside until you get to the end.

How to find Scripture references

The Scripture quotes in this book are taken from the Bible, God's Holy Word, and have been placed at the back of the book to make it easier to read for people who are not familiar with the Bible. You can find these references easily by using the search function on your computer (Control F) and typing in the chapter heading.

Or you can download the references here and place them alongside you when you read this book. The url for the download can be found under the heading References.

These references have been provided so that readers can do their own research using their preferred Bible translation.

Occasional paraphrasing
To get the message across succinctly for readers who are not familiar with the Bible, occasionally I've paraphrased Scripture 'the Aussie way.' At the same time I provide the full Scripture reference so that you can look up the verse in your favourite translation.

Occasional shortening
I may also shorten the Scripture verse for clarity's sake, but will provide the full references in the appendix. This may not be politically correct but is done to improve the readability of this study.

The Bible has always been the number one bestselling book in the world and billions of copies of this, history book of the Jewish people circulate.

There are good reasons for that.

How-to instruction manual

Some of the reasons are that this history book of the Jewish people is also called 'The Truth' and doubles as a how-to and how-not-to instruction manual for living a productive and fulfilling life for the whole of humanity.

The focus of this book is to find out what true love is and 'how-to love' according to The Father and His Son.

At the end of the book there are **resources and examples** which will help you do your own research.

The Book of Truth
I will tell you what is written in
The Book of Truth.
(Daniel 10:21)

Next: Chapter One

How To Describe Love

CHAPTER ONE
How to Describe Love

"The greatest happiness of life is the conviction that we are loved; loved for ourselves, or rather, loved in spite of ourselves." Victor Hugo

First we have a look at how 'love' is described in ordinary life. After this we'll see what The Holy Word has to say about it.

Smiles and winks

Two of my best friends, Doreen and Jim, have been married for fifty-nine years this summer. Everytime I think about them I feel warm and fuzzy.

When I asked them to describe love, Doreen answered without thinking about it for even a second, 'Growing old together and smiling at each other every morning after waking up.' She nodded affirmatively, as did Jim, who added, 'And I'll give her a wink, every night, before going to sleep.'

I love that; growing old together, smiling at each other, every day, and a wink at night. There is so much that is unspoken in those words that speaks volumes, and it is all good.

It is impossible to force a genuine smile.

It sounds like Doreen and Jim love each other fearlessly.

Clearly my friends Doreen and Jim treat each other with respect and enjoy being in each other's company, even after all those years.

See, I'm intensely looking for a template because in the environment that I grew up in, the opposite happened. All through the generations we've had alcoholism, violence, mental illness, and abuse.

It took me a while to figure out that not all people grow up like that. I didn't dare speak up much either, because for sure I would have been considered a tattletale.

Now that the older generations have passed away and I am in the process of becoming an elder myself, it is my duty to speak up and aim for my generation and the ones that come after me to do better.

Up until I welcomed the Father and His Son into my life, I had no reference points nor templates for a kind and truly loving relationship.

When your name is safe

Another wonderful way that I've heard love described was by a little child. When the 7-year-old was asked what she thought love was all about, she wrinkled her nose and stated with authority that, 'Love is when your name is safe in someone's mouth.'

I'll definitely go with that one and will do my very best to keep everyone's name safe in my mouth.

Without a doubt, that is what Jesus meant when he reiterated His Father's' Word and said that we are to love each other and not to speak idle words or call anyone a fool.

Control your tongue

In James 3 a whole chapter is devoted to being in control of your tongue, which is described as an unruly evil, full of deadly poison that sets on the fire of hell. Ouch.

As a child I was sometimes put in my place and told that 'words can hurt.'

I cannot recall why this was so, but certainly found out later in life how it hurts when people spoke harshly to me or school 'friends' whispered and giggled behind my back.

Steer the traffic of our words

My friend Michal Stawicki puts it beautifully in his new book, *Power up Your Self Talk*, where he mentions that we are to *'steer the traffic of our words.'* I couldn't have said it any better myself. Michal's words are a good reminder to be careful of what comes out of our mouth. And this goes both ways. We have to be careful how we address others as well as how we address ourselves.

Next, we'll address what God's Holy Word has to say about love.

Our Father in heaven sets us an example of being merciful, gracious, patient, loving, truthful, forgiving, and just. And we were made in His likeness. This means that we are able to live up to His standard.

Made in God's image

God created man in his own image, in the image of God created he him; male and female created He them.
(Genesis 1:27)

It's good to remember that the easiest and quickest way for us to be 'unloving' to one another often enough is with the words that come out of our mouth.

34

Don't speak idle words

*Every idle word that you shall speak,
you shall have to give account of this on the
day of judgment.*
(Matthew 12:36)

Next: Chapter Two

What Does the Holy Word Say About Love?

CHAPTER TWO

What Does the Holy Word Say About Love?

I command you to love one another.
(John 15:17)

When I started to read the Bible in earnest I noticed that we are 'commanded' to love each other.

I used to think that, well you know, some people we love and others we don't. Simply because some people are lovable and others aren't. Not so, according to Scripture; just get over yourselves and love each other already.

The word 'love' and variants thereof are mentioned 442 times in the King James Bible, 545 times in the Amplified Bible and 686 times in the New International Version. That's a lot of times!

I won't be addressing each Scripture verse with the word 'love' in it. We'll look at the Scripture verses that tell us 'how to love' and the ones that explain what 'true love' is.

Love one another

We'll start with the command, not a request but a command from Jesus, to love each other;

"... Love one another. As I have loved you, so you must love one another." (John 13:34-35)

See, we're not given a choice. It's a command. Similar messages were given by Moses. He told us 'not to retaliate or hold grudges but to love our neighbours as we love ourselves.'

Jesus mentions that His disciples will be recognised by the love they have for one another.

And exactly the same rule applies for the foreigners: Treat them as if they are your own and love them as yourself.

Many of us aren't that keen on anything unfamiliar, but we're clearly told to love others as we love ourselves.

My family is in the habit of welcoming new neighbours to our neighbourhood with a bunch of muffins or a lunch invite. It is a great way to get to know each other. It works both ways and is even a little selfish, because in my family we'll grab any excuse for a friendly get-together.

Talk is cheap. The Bible tells us to take care of each other. Period. Later on I'll give you real life examples of true love.

From the beginning… love each other
The message you heard from the very beginning is this: we must love one another.
(1 John 3:11)

Next: Chapter Three

Jesus Personified Love

CHAPTER THREE
Jesus Personified Love

*The greatest love of all is to sacrifice one's life
for one's friends.*
(John 15:13)

Jesus taught us in many different ways what love was all about. Jesus told us not to say bad things about each other and He repeated his Father's Word when He stated that the message we heard from the very beginning is that we must love each other.

Jesus personified love. He said that the greatest love of all is to give your life for your friends.

Jesus proceeded to do just that when he sacrificed his life for the sake of others. Jesus didn't just tell us what to do, he showed us in action and then invited us to follow Him.

Jesus sacrificed his life for us so that we may live. He died very young, in his early thirties. Most of us hope to live much longer than that.

What happened?
What many people overlook is 'how come' that Jesus laid down his life for us? What happened?

41

Did he want to do this? No! When Jesus' time came, he sweat great drops of blood and he asked His Father THREE times to please not have to suffer like this. But Jesus added to his desperate plea; 'However, Father, may your will be done.'

It is fair to say that Jesus experienced a lot of pain and stress, but this didn't stop him. He repeatedly asked to be let off but despite his extreme distress, continued on.

Marcu Pontius Pilate, governor of Judea (26 - 36 ce) reluctantly, when pressured, sent Jesus to his death. He washed his hands saying, 'I find in him no fault at all.'

When Pilate asked Jesus if he was a king, Jesus answered,

Bear witness to the truth
You say that I am a king. To this end was I born, and for this cause came I into the world, that I should bear witness unto the truth. Every one that is of the truth heareth my voice.
(John 18:37)

Why was Jesus born? To bear witness to the truth. What is the truth? God's Word is also known as 'The Scripture of Truth.'

The Word made flesh (Saviour)

Jesus became the living word. The Bible tells us that 'The Word was made flesh' which meant that Jesus lived according to His Father's will and instructions as a perfect example for us to follow.

Jesus is our salvation

The name Jesus (IPA: /ˈdʒiːzəs/) is derived from the name Iēsous (Greek: Ἰησοῦς), the Greek form of the Hebrew name Yeshua (Hebrew: ישוע). As its roots lie in the name Yeshua, it is etymologically related to another biblical name, Joshua.

The Hebrew Bible uses Yehoshua (יְהוֹשֻׁעַ) for Joshua, which means "Yah is Salvation." Many nowadays reject the term Yahshua (יהשע) in favor of Yeshua (ישוע) as the original pronunciation.

Save people from their sins

Whichever way you look at it, Jesus' name means 'Saviour' and He was born to save people from their sins by showing them how it is done.

What does it mean, 'to save people from their sins?' What is a sin?

43

Sin is lawlessness
Everyone who *practices sin practices lawlessness as well. Indeed, sin is lawlessness… in Jesus there is no sin…*
(1 John 3:4)

Wrongdoing is sin
All *wrongdoing is called sin…*
(1 John 5:17)

According to Scripture sinning is equal to lawlessness. People who sin break the law. Lawbreakers equals sinners. Which law? God's law. We'll get to this later.

Sinning is of the devil
Those who keep *sinning are of the devil, because the devil has been sinning from the beginning. The reason the Son of God appeared was to destroy the devil's work. (1 John 3:8)*

How would we even know what is the right way unless we have a law which tells us the right way, and an example to follow?

Save people from their sins
And she shall give birth to a son, and you shall call his name YESHUA (Jesus): for he shall

save his people from their sins.
(Matthew 1:21)

Next: Chapter Four

Why Was Jesus Crucified?

CHAPTER FOUR
Why Was Jesus Crucified?
TRUE LOVE

*Pilate said… I find in him no fault at all.
I find no fault in him… I find no fault in him…
The King of the Jews… I am innocent of the
blood of this just person... (John 17:38, John
19:4-6, Matthew 27:24)*

So why was Jesus crucified? He was crucified because his sinless life exposed the hypocrisy of those around him. It was because of Jesus that his contemporaries weren't any longer able to cover up their indiscretions.

The easiest way for those around Jesus to be able to continue their sinful lives was to get rid of Him.

Pilates, the governor of Judea attested to Jesus' innocence.

Jesus was born because
Sure, it is also true that:

- God gave His Son so that we may have eternal life.

47

- Jesus gave his life as a ransom for many.
- Jesus was born to bear witness to the truth.
- Who believes in Jesus will live forever, even though he dies.
- Believers are called the children of God.
- Jesus was an atoning sacrifice for our sins.

But the worldly, earthly reason that Jesus was sacrificed was that he had gotten up the nose of those (clergy) who liked to think of themselves as the 'Keepers of the Truth.' Pharisees and the like. They were anything but, as Jesus came to show them.

Why do you hate me so much?
Many good works did I show you
from my Father; for which of those
works do you stone me?
(John 10:32)

TRUE LOVE

God's love
This is how God's love was revealed among us; that He sent His one and only Son into the world so that we might live through Him.

True love
This is true love; not that we loved God, but that he loved us and sent his Son as a sacrifice to take away our sins.
(1 John 4:9-10)

Both Jesus and the Father show us true love; The Father by sacrificing His Son and the Son by obeying His Father, and in doing so, sacrificing His life for us.

Now we know what true love is, but people get sidetracked by these wonderful Scripture verses and lose the bigger picture of what happened when Jesus was crucified and what this means for humanity.

Sacrificial lamb
Ultimately what happened in real life was that Jesus' very existence, his sinless life, his innocence and good deeds, made people aware of their own sins and they couldn't stand it and crucified Him because of it.

The lamb of God
'... Look, the Lamb of God,
which takes away the sin of the world.'
(John 1:29)

Jesus' innocence and sacrifice testifies of his love for us. It meant that he placed God first in His life and would never take His Father's name in vain for any reason. It meant that he had no idols and kept the Sabbath holy in the way it was intended. Not how it was kept by the Pharisees but how it was intended to be kept as stipulated by His Heavenly Father.

It meant that Jesus honoured his parents and elders. He didn't commit adultery. He did not kill, lie, steal or covet.

Jesus treated God and all those made in God's image with respect. He didn't need to come up with excuses for lying, killing, stealing, or blaspheming because he stuck to the law. That meant that Jesus was without sin. 1 John 3:5

Jesus knew that His Father always heard Him. Why was that?

God hears and helps good people
When good people cry, God hears them and delivers them out of all their troubles.
(Psalm 34:17)

Because Jesus was sinless and our Father hears good people. He doesn't hear sinners; those who break His Law.

Only an innocent person like Jesus would be able to be that atoning sacrifice to cleanse our sins.

No cover for their sin
If I had not come and spoken unto them, they had not had sin: but now they have no cover for their sin.
(John 15:22)

Next: Chapter Five

How Does Sin Play Out in Our Own Life?

CHAPTER FIVE

How Does Sin Play Out in Our Own Life?

Nay: but, except ye repent,
ye shall all likewise perish.
(Luke 13:1-9)

...I will punish you according to the fruit of your
deeds, said the LORD...
(Jeremiah 21:14)

Most of us think that we're doing just fine. This happens because we measure ourselves up against the people around us instead of measuring against the standard set by Our Father and His Son.

Whose standard do we live by?
Here's how this may play out in our own life.

Example One - do not swear
The words coming out of your mouth even hurt your own ears. Your thumb is doubling in size in front of your eyes. That rotten wind slammed the door right on your hand. Your toddler is staring at you with her mouth wide open. Oh, never mind, just add a few coins to the cussing jar and she'll be right.

And that promise I made the other day, I'll get to it... one day.

Example Two - do not steal
'No one will notice,' you tell yourself, as you fill your bag with notepads and pencils from the office. 'If they paid you enough, you wouldn't have to help yourself to stationary. It's only fair that the office supplies your home with pens and paper.' You actually manage to convince yourself that you're entitled to things that don't belong to you.

Example Three - do not lie - honour your parents
It's just a little fib. Mum would only get worried if she knew you would be hanging out with this crowd. What she doesn't know doesn't hurt her. Right?

Example Four - do not commit adultery
If he/she would pay you more attention you wouldn't feel the need to have this late night supper with your accountant. The kids always get in the way. Your accountant is stroking your arm and whispering sweet nothings into your ear. You're entitled to some loving, darn it!

Inappropriate? Very much so. Do we want to hear about it? Not really. Most people don't like the moralistic talk. It is not 'worldly.' It is a case of, 'I won't criticize you if you leave me alone.'

'Don't expose my sin and I won't expose yours.'

Peer pressure can turn many of us into sinners.

Example Five - do not covet
Your clothes are bursting out of your wardrobe and you recently bought another rack to fit all your clothes that won't fit in the wardrobe. There's a party at the weekend and you find yourself in the shops looking for another outfit. The last thing you need is more clothes, but here we go again.

Example Six - honour God only
Have you ever been to church and been made to feel bad about certain Biblical understandings, insights and revelations that you have come to? Has it ever occurred to you that where lots of people gather, situations are created where commandments of men are adhered to instead of God's commandments, and the lowest common denominator prevails?

Follow the Good Shepherd
Jesus called us his flock. As sheep we're supposed to be following the Good Shepherd.

Going to church may help us do so. Going to church carries a risk. And the risk is that we might be dumbed down and made to accept the status quo as set by the church. What the church preaches is not always in line with what God's Word teaches us.

Let's face it, as people we are like herd animals who like to hang out together and few of us are prepared to rock the boat if this means that we're not going to be popular. Be that at the club, the pub, school, at work, or the church.

Too often we may just follow the status quo and guidelines set by man, even though we know it is wrong. I know that I do, more often than I like to admit.

> *"How can they continue serving this person alcohol? He/she can barely walk anymore.*
>
> *I daren't say anything because when my buddy did the other week he was blocked from the Club."*
>
> *"I cannot stand these bullies. Pff, at least they're not targeting me. I'll get out of the way quickly and stay quiet so I won't get hassled."*

"This is an eco-friendly registered resort that should not be cleaning their bathrooms with bleach. But if I create a fuss, I'll lose my job."

"God says that we are to celebrate His Feasts, but my church tells me that is outdated information. I can read, however, and I know that God would like us to celebrate His Feasts. They'll kick me out if I insist."

I know from experience that sticking with Biblical principles can get people excommunicated from their church. If people disagree with Catholic church doctrine they'll be called a heretic and be thrown out of the church.

In vain they worship me
But in vain they do worship me, teaching for doctrines the commandments of men.
(Matthew 15:9)

Forgotten the law of God
My people are destroyed for lack of knowledge. Because you have rejected knowledge, I will also reject you as My priests. Since you have forgotten the law of your God, I will also forget your children.
(Hosea 4:6)

Both our Father and His Son strongly rejected the doctrine of mainstream clergy.

What makes us think that what mainstream rabbis and ministers are preaching today is any different, and more in line with God's will than it was in Biblical times?

In 2019, according to *ABC's Australia Talks National Survey*, Religious leaders were distrusted by a full 70 percent of the population, with 35 percent saying they did not trust them "at all." And even within their own flocks, religious leaders were viewed with some suspicion.

WHAT IS TRUE LOVE? ACCORDING TO THE BIBLE

We know that clergy are supposed to be living and teaching according to God's Holy Word and we also know that often they don't.

Of course the majority of churches and pastors aim for their parishioners to have a close relationship with our Heavenly Father.

Churches are great places for fellowship and communion and I'm grateful that pastors put themselves out there to provide these opportunities, and the environment for believers to hang out and support one and other.

We cannot expect to agree with everything that is said in church in the same way that we cannot expect to agree with everything that is said by people outside the church either.

I'm impressed with the church I have been visiting for the last few months, because the pastors focus on the relationship between parishioners as well as the relationship we have with our Heavenly Father and His Son.

We always come away refreshed and encouraged from these local church services where the pastors teach according to the Bible and that's why I asked for the pastors to write a foreword.

Next: Chapter Six

Don't Get Sucked In By The Silent Majority

CHAPTER SIX

Don't Get Sucked in by the Silent Majority

The duty of the priest is to teach knowledge of good and evil but you have lost your way and caused many to stumble into sin… you have violated the covenant… (Malachi 2:7-9)

For laying aside the commandment of God, ye hold the tradition of men, as the washing of pots and cups: and many other such like things ye do.
(Mark 7:8)

For instance, I hear church-goers say that all of us have sinned, and this is certainly true for me; however, Apostle John is talking about the past here.

If we claim we have not sinned,
we make Him out to be a liar
and His word is not in us.
(1 John 1:10)

Once we know Jesus and have an example to follow, we're supposed to do better.

Walk as He walked
*He that saith he abideth in him
ought himself also so to walk,
even as he walked.
(1 John 2:6)*

Is everyone a sinner?

Abraham obeyed God
I know that in various places in the Bible it is
mentioned that everyone is a sinner. However,
as you will read in my next book, Abraham and
his offspring were blessed by God because
Abraham obeyed God's voice, he did as he was
told, kept God's commandments, his legislation,
and His laws. Doesn't sound like a sinner to me.

Noah was just and perfect
Noah and his family were saved from the flood,
because Noah was just and perfect and walked
with God. The same word is used for Noah as
was used for Jesus by Pilate, 'just.' Noah doesn't
sound like a sinner to me either.

Caleb and Joshua did as they were told
Millions died in the desert but Caleb and Joshua
were saved because they did as their heavenly
Father told them.

Highly unlikely that our Father would let millions perish and save two sinners.

Our Father didn't think that everyone is a sinner or He would not have singled out and saved those faithful and loyal men such as Abraham, Noah, Caleb and Joshua.

You can read more about faithful followers in the next book of the 'Love, Truth & God Series;' Book three, 'The Core Message of the Bible in a Few Pages; The Truth About The Good News.'

In Jesus' time mention was made of the parents of John the Baptist, Zechariah and his wife Elizabeth, as righteous people.

Both righteous… blameless
And they were both righteous before God, walking in all the commandments and ordinances of the Lord blameless.
(Luke 1:6)

Jesus came to call sinners to repent
Jesus did not think that everyone had sinned either. He said that 'he did not come to heal the innocent (δίκαιος, ία, ιον dikaios: correct, righteous, by impl. innocent) but he came to call sinners to repent.' Clearly Jesus recognised two

63

different groups of people: sinners and innocent people.

He told people, after he healed them, to 'sin no more.'

Stop sinning
There was one particular disabled guy in Jerusalem who had been ill for thirty-eight years. After Jesus healed him He said, 'You are better now, stop sinning so that nothing worse will happen to you.'

More joy over one sinner than ninety nine good ones
Jesus said that 'heaven rejoices more over one bad person that turns good than over ninety-nine people that behave themselves.'

The difference between weeds and wheat
In many parables Jesus separated out those who did good, and those who did not. For instance, in the parable where he mentioned not to worry about the weeds.

Jesus said to let the weeds grow together with the wheat and separate them out at harvest time when the weeds will be tied in bundles and burned. After this the wheat will be gathered in the barn.

When Jesus mentioned the wheat he was obviously referring to the good stuff. And weed; we all know what weeds are like.

Seed bearing much fruit
Jesus also told the parable of the sower where he gave examples of seed not producing due to falling into stony places an amongst thorns, as opposed to seed falling into good ground and bearing much fruit.

Sheep and goats
Jesus mentioned gathering all nations and separating them from another as a shepherd divides his sheep from the goats. He said those that did not help others when they needed help will be punished and the good (innocent, δίκαιος, ία, ιον, just, in the eyes of God, those who live up to his standard) will live forever.

With the Samaritan story Jesus clarified that a good person is someone who takes care of others, even complete strangers, regardless of religion.

It's not about religion
With these parables that I just mentioned, Jesus was not talking about believers versus unbelievers. You can believe all you like, but if

you do the wrong thing by others… who cares that you believe in Jesus?

During our last move I booked a 'Christian' removalist. He advertised as such on his website. Whilst I was at death's door in the hospital he tried to extort an extra six or eight hundred dollars from my daughters. In the end, we never received the contents of my garage, which was filled to the brim with goods.

This removalist called himself a 'Christian', but he did not act like one.

Jesus was not talking about 'Christians versus non-Christians,' or 'church-goers versus non-church goers.' Jesus was talking about good people versus bad people. Sinners versus decent people.

With these sayings Jesus clearly separated out the ones with sin and those without. He wouldn't tell us 'to sin no more,' if this were not possible for us.

He himself lived a sin-free life as an example for us. Clearly, as the parables above show us, Jesus knew plenty of people that did not sin and He stated that it is possible for us not to sin.

Be perfect

Be perfect, therefore, as your Heavenly Father
is perfect.
(Matthew 5:48)

Be holy

"Speak to the entire congregation of the
Israelites and tell them: 'Be holy because I, the
LORD your God, am holy. (Leviticus 19:2)

Don't get sucked in

Don't get sucked in by the silent majority, where everyone agrees that we're all sinners and no one criticizes one another and everyone just does what is right in their own eyes.

Sure, at some stage we all 'were' sinners. But the whole idea of following Jesus is that we can start with a clean slate.

No sin in Jesus - stop sinning

You know that Christ came to take away sins,
and in Him there is no sin. No one who lives in
union with Him keeps on sinning. Everyone
who continues to sin has not seen Him or
known Him.
(1 John 3:5-6)

Stop saying and believing that everyone is a sinner. It is a pharisaical expression designed to lead everyone astray and not true (according to our Father and His Son), as I just showed you.

If you keep saying that everyone is a sinner, that implies that you've given up before you even got going. It implies that you don't know Jesus.

No one who lives in union with Jesus, no one who has met and recognised Him, keeps on sinning. Everyone who continues to sin has not seen Him or known Him.

Yes, there are false prophets in the Bible. Jesus warned us against them. Don't listen to them.

When I was little, a family member used to say to me; 'Are you so holy then?' At the time that reliably used to shut me up. Now I wished that I would have responded with; 'I'm practising and with my Father's help, I will get there.'

Be perfect, be holy
Jesus said, 'Be perfect.' His Father said, 'Be holy.' They wouldn't say that if it weren't possible for us to follow their command.

You promised to help someone, do it! You want to be better; go for it! It is not as hard as you think to be a kind and loving person. If you find it hard, pray for help.

The Lord heard me and saved me

I prayed to the Lord and He heard me and saved me out of all my troubles.
(Psalm 34:6)

I will give you rest

Come to me when you're tired and bent over, under the weight of your problems. I will give you rest.

Do what I tell you and learn from me. I am kind, patient and modest. I'll help you find inner peace.

What I'll tell you to do will be easy and not too hard or difficult for you.
(Matthew 11:28-30)

Next: Chapter Seven

The meaning of Jesus' Crucifiction

CHAPTER SEVEN
The Meaning of Jesus' Crucifixion

This is the verdict:
The Light has come into the world, but men loved the darkness rather than the Light, because their deeds were evil.
(John 3:19)

The true meaning of why Jesus was crucified is because he was an example to us. He showed us how to live a sinless life, and showed us what we are to do when we answer his call; how to follow Him. Jesus showed us a perfect example of true love.

Watered down message
Many churches water this message down because they're afraid to scare people away if the true message is revealed.

Instead we're told to just accept Jesus in our heart, repent of our sins, ask for forgiveness, and He'll work in us and through us.

71

Cause we're all sinners, right? And this is the best we can do? It just isn't that fashionable nowadays trying to be a good person.

Oh, guess what? It never was.

Jesus was killed because He was a good person.

So, yes, just the same, it's a jolly good idea to invite Jesus in your heart and ask Him to replace your stony heart with a flesh one.

To start your new life; pray as follows
If you want to do this, you can pray,

> *Father, who made heaven and earth and everything it contains, you know everything from the very beginning till the very end. Thank you for being so loving and magnanimous to be paying attention to me, forgiving me for all the bad decisions that I've made and the bad actions I have taken and saving me out of all my troubles.*
>
> *Thank you, Jesus, for helping me transform my life for the better. I'm sorry I mucked up, I promise to make up where I can and do better. Please forgive me for my muck-ups and thank you for cleansing my heart and directing my steps from now on.*

I know that you will give me rest and inner peace and that what you'll tell me to do will not be too hard or difficult for me.

Done!

From experience I know that this works for sure.

And while you're at it, read the whole of Psalm 25, which reminds us of God's love and mercy.

Remember me according to your love
Don't remember the sins of my youth, nor my disobedience: according to your love and mercy remember me please, O LORD. (Psalm 25:7)

However, is this really all there is to it?

Will just faith get me there?
In the Book of James we're told that faith without evidence means nothing. What kind of evidence are we looking for?

James mentions that having faith develops patience. Having patience means that we feel whole and perfect without coveting and always wanting something.

James tells us to not be double minded and he tells the humble and poor to rejoice.

73

James also tells us to be a doer of the word instead of just a hearer.

Blessings for doers

If you look closely into the perfect law that sets people free, and keep on paying attention to it and do not simply listen and then forget it, but put it into practice; you will be blessed by God in what you do. (James 1:22-25)

We're given free will. And as such it helps to know what is expected from us in as much detail as possible.

If we're for real, when we call ourselves 'Christians,' we're supposed to be following the directions that are given to us in the Bible.

When we're hanging out with family, friends, and colleagues, are we sticking to our guns when the majority insists that we travel along the (lawless) broad way?

Expect to lose friends when you decide to travel that narrow road. It tends to be rather quiet on that narrow path.

How to lay down our life?

Are we prepared to lay down our lives for our friends and stay with what we know to be true even though this could ruin our life as we know it, or even kill us?

What does it mean to lay down our life? We lay down our lives when we live our lives for the benefit of others instead of for our own joy and gratification.

Laying down one's life is about being that shiny example, service, sacrifice with integrity. Will we keep our integrity every step of the way or will we sell our soul?

Israel Folau is a perfect present day example of a person who's willing to give up his life for his belief.

Israel is an Australian professional rugby player whose multi-million-dollar-contract was terminated because he quoted from the Bible and refused to retract this quote when people were offended by it.

From Israel's Facebook thread below:
Excited to continue my journey with the Qantas Wallabies Waratahs for another four seasons! Big year ahead, can't wait to get started with the boys. All glory to my Lord Jesus Christ, without him none of this would be possible. Everything that I've achieved is through the power and

strength of God. #ILiveAndPlayForChrist #Wallabies #NSWWaratahs February 9, 2019

When your career is at stake and millions of dollars can be lost, will you bail or stick with The Truth and continue being that shining example?

Israel puts his money where his mouth is. Israel is being misjudged by many as being judgmental, whereas he merely quoted Scripture. He is not the author of the Scripture Verses he quoted.
It's irrelevant if we agree or disagree with Israel because it is not about him. If we disagree with the Scripture he quoted, take it up with the Big Boss. Argue with, and talk to Him who inspired the writing.

When we look for examples in real life we'll find them, such as Israel Folau, and for instance the younger brother of Hollywood megastar Alec Baldwin, Stephen Baldwin, who has become well-known for his devout Christian faith.

Stephen is known as a 'Jesus freak' in the industry and misses out on roles because of his faith.

> *"It's unfortunate that because I have believed in Jesus for 15 years that there are*

many in Hollywood who are unwilling to work with me. That's not a guess. Casting people and producers have told me that they've brought up my name in a room and the response was, "No way, we're not bringing that guy and his Bible over here."

Public figures who experienced a spiritual rebirth are Chuck Norris, Bob Dylan, Mr. T, George Bush, Jane Fonda, Bono, Alice Cooper, Johnny Cash, John Foreman, Kirk Cameron, and recently Kayne West, just to name a few.

Dolly Parton says, *"In my faith, it bothers me sometimes when I see people worshiping the stars and all that. I'm like, Oh Lord, don't ever let me go there. That's why I want to ship that one up to God.*

I don't need nobody worshiping me," she added. "If I do shine and radiate, I'd like to think that is God's light and I'd like to pass that on. I want to direct people to Him, not me."

Dolly's sentiments are in line with His Holy Word from (Matthew 5:16.)

Let your light shine
Let your light shine before men..

I don't necessarily agree with all the lifestyles, philosophies or theological practices of people experiencing rebirth and/or who call themselves Christians. But I have an appreciation for anyone who is committed to their Christian faith and is happy to let the world know what family they belong to.

Jesus openly spoke about His Father and the gospel wherever he went and He said,

Proudly acknowledge the Son of God
Whoever will be ashamed of me and of my words, of him will the Son of Man be ashamed, when he comes in his glory, and the glory of the Father, and of the holy angels.
(Luke 9:26)

"Everyone who acknowledges me before men, the Son of Man will also acknowledge before the angels of God;

but he who denies me in the presence of men will be denied in the presence of God's angels."
(Luke 12:8-9)

When we look for shining 'Christian' examples we can find them, but they are more often than not, quietly working and supporting in the background.

Sticking with it.
It is a common theme in society to replace aging partners with younger ones and to bail when children have medical problems that put a strain on the marriage.

Sticking with it, not bailing out, is laying down your life for your friends.

When your partner falls ill, and the business falls in a heap… will you support your bestie through this? Through thick and thin… till death do us part? Or will you bail and find someone else to hang out with instead?

Will you tell 'little' fibs in order to get away with things?

Sticking together
The story of Ruth and Naomi, which you can find in the Bible in *The Book of Ruth*, is a heartwarming story of two women who stuck together through thick and thin and came out pretty good. Ruth turned out to be one of Jesus' ancestors.

Where you go I will go
"Don't ask me to leave you. Where you go, I will go and where you sleep, I will sleep. Your people are my people and your God is my

God... I pray that only death will be able to separate us."
(Ruth 1:16-18)

Follow promptings from the Holy Spirit

One of our friends, David, volunteered at a radio station and played all kinds of songs during his breakfast shows.

Slowly the Holy Spirit worked through David and showed him that songs such as AC/DC's 'Highway to Hell' and similar ones aren't the way to go.

He changed the tune of his shows, much to the chagrin of the radio station.

This young man eventually left because he was made to feel unwelcome after he decided to play more wholesome music.

David, however, kept his integrity. He looked forward to these weekly sessions, had a following, and enjoyed the radio scene.

Yet he did not sell out and did not yield to the pressure to continue playing the popular rock and roll songs. It cost him dearly.

From being a popular Drive Time Show Presenter, he then did not play music for quite some time.

But David followed his conscience, which told him that these songs aren't conducive to living a wholesome life.

And even though it took awhile for him to find his feet again, he persevered and did not relapse back into playing music that did not agree with the whisperings of the Holy Spirit and his newfound understandings.

David decided to do 'the right thing' instead of doing 'the popular thing' or 'the easy thing.'

Don't sell your soul
Whatever you do, don't sell your soul.

What to give in exchange for one's soul?
For what is a man profited,
if he shall gain the whole world,
and lose his own soul?
or what shall a man give in
exchange for his soul?
(Matthew 16:26)

Next: Chapter Eight

Jesus Sets The Standard

CHAPTER EIGHT
Jesus Sets the Standard

Everyone who does evil hates the Light, and does not come into the Light for fear that his deeds will be exposed.
But whoever practices the truth comes into the Light…
(John 3:20-21)

What I like about Jesus and why He is my number One mentor is because Jesus didn't only tell us what to do, but He showed us as well. Jesus did the right thing all of his life. He did what was right, instead of the popular or easy thing. He didn't sin and He healed *'everyone'* that was brought to Him or that came to Him. Incredible! I don't know a physician or minister quite like that.

Jesus paid a high price
What I don't like so much is the fact that doing the right thing cost Jesus His (earthly) life.

So now I'm following Jesus. Has my life as I know it disappeared? Yes, it has been completely transformed! There is nothing left of my old life, other than my faith, which tells me that trusting in the Lord and His Son will get me to where I need to be.

83

We're in the process of slowly rebuilding my life and it is better now than I could ever have imagined.

The place I live in is a dream, I'm surrounded by positive supporting people, have become the author of multiple books, and my health is improving as we speak.

Do I sin? I'm certainly a work in progress, and every day I am becoming more aware of how to make a positive, instead of a negative impact.

Am I healing everyone that I come across? If only. Haha, I do my best by pointing to HIM as much as I can.

Jesus set us a standard to live by.
It is only because we have standards to live by that we know what is right and wrong.

Love each other as you love yourself. Sure, but as mentioned earlier, you wouldn't know how to be loving towards others if you're not very loving toward yourself, and if you were to apply this principle to greeting one another you could get into trouble.

Self Love and self-care are important because without it we aren't able to help others to the best of our abilities. I know, I tried, and it does not work.

Love your life and lose it, hate it and keep it
Why would Jesus have said that "anyone who loves their life will lose it, while anyone who hates their life in this world will keep it for eternal life?" (John 12:25)

It's fair to say that Jesus wouldn't have liked his life very much. All throughout his ministry, he was accused of evil deeds, even though he did the opposite. His family did not seem to understand Him whilst he was alive. His fellow parishioners attempted to stone Him and throw him down a hill. On more than one occasion he had to run for his life.

He was crucified because he was a good person, and at the end of his life, everyone, including all his disciples, denied and deserted Him.

If we're following in Jesus' footsteps we have to understand that not everyone will love us, and hating our life is fine. Hating your brother/sister however will get you in BIG trouble.

I know churchgoers who have faithfully attended church for thirty years or more and they have never heard of this Scripture verse. You don't have to know about Scripture to live a decent life, but it helps.

At some stage, I was chatting with a friend who had been a church-going parishioner all her life. But she didn't like it much when I, just once in a blue moon, referred to a Scripture verse. She asked me, 'Why wouldn't I just read a novel or a thriller so that we can discuss that?'

I explained to her that I live in Bonus-time now, since our Father saved me and kept me alive after several medical emergencies. I couldn't bear to spend even a moment of this precious time that I've been given and 'waste my time away' by reading thrillers and novels.

I am not saying that there is anything wrong with reading thrillers or novels. Clearly, this is a very popular pastime for millions of people, and no doubt gives many people much-needed relaxation time and relief from stressful jobs and/or family circumstances, etc.

For me, however, it would be a waste of time.

I give this as an example. Do not judge. Everyone's situation is different. What is right for one person can be wrong for another. But all of us in our hearts know what the right thing to do is.

Doing the right thing is not always easy. Usually, there is opposition and it requires strength and character to keep walking that narrow path instead of following along with the majority on the broad way.

To please my friend I could have started to read the novels she suggested but that would have been the wrong thing to do for me.

Do not love this world
Genuine loving and kind, compassionate people tend to hate this world filled with corruption, poverty, and misery. They often volunteer and donate their time and money to try and make this world a better place.

People who love life and this world are often living a cushy existence.

They don't necessarily go much out of their way to help those who are less fortunate.

Obviously, I'm generalising here and there are always exceptions. But look in your heart and around you and you'll see what I mean.

Jesus did not save up to build an extension to his house. He didn't have a house.

He did not have a wardrobe filled with rows of garments. After he died, he only left behind the clothes he wore.

I'm working on it. As I'm writing this down I'm ashamed to admit that, like most girls, I like clothes. Nothing wrong with that, but I also collect them. Too many of them.

John the Baptist told us that if we have two coats we should share with those who have none, and the same with food.

Feed The Hungry is one of my favourite organisations, where a mere $30 feeds five children for a whole month!

I was so happy when I read 'not to love this world.' I never had, other than clothes, of course.

But here I found confirmation, which gave me much comfort.

Do not love the world

Do not love the world nor the things in the world. If anyone loves the world, the love of the Father is not in him... The world is passing away, and also its lusts; but those who do the will of God live forever. (1 John 2:15-17)

Next: Chapter Nine

True Love In Action

CHAPTER NINE
True Love in Action

God so loved the world that He gave His one and only Son, that everyone who believes in Him shall not perish but have eternal life. For God did not send His Son into the world to condemn the world, but to save the world through Him...
(John 3:1-17)

If you keep My commandments, you will remain in My love…
(John 15:9-11)

True love in action
I'll tell you about true love in action. About keeping someone's name safe in one's mouth. About keeping smiling, even when the going gets tough.

EXAMPLE ONE
The other day I spoke to a disability support worker, Lisa, who casually mentioned that she and her sister Anne had been their Mum's sole support for the last ten years. This was one of the requirements under the Australian Balance of Family Test for entry and permanent stay in Australia for their Mum. That's a huge

commitment and without a doubt impacted the lives of her and her sister greatly, yet she mentioned it with a smile and matter of factly. It didn't really appear to be a choice, but more a natural thing to do, to get Mum transferred from South Africa to live with her daughters in Australia.

I know many people who don't even know the name of the nursing home of their Mum or Dad, but these two middle-aged women organised transport for their Mum from the other side of the world and did, and are doing, whatever they can to keep their parent safe, healthy, and comfortable.

EXAMPLE TWO
When a medical emergency had me at death's door, I was fortunate enough to have family members who took care of me after I became seriously ill.

They didn't bail and run. They stayed around and with the help of Our Father and His Son, nursed me back to health.

How easy would it have been for these young adults to say, 'See you later, we're off to have a life.'

They didn't. They didn't wince and whine, nor did they spill around all the gory details of what happened to me.

Instead, they sprung into action. One of them sat up at night and phoned around to get hold of specialists and surgeons for better diagnosis and treatment for my medical emergency.

(You can read more about this in my books '*My Story of Survival*' and '*God Healed Me.*')

Suffice it to say that neither of those two young adults packed up and ran.

The eldest got a job real quick and supported our household financially through this medical emergency. Whilst the youngest studied disability care as well as took care of the household for all of us whilst nursing me back to health.

Both of them wouldn't have loved their life at this particular point. They laid it down for their Mum to support her and be there for her.

Sounds like this is the right thing to do? You betcha! This is called true love.

How many people actually do this? I have experienced the opposite also, as many of us have.

I've been shown true love in action. How blessed am I?

This is what Jesus spoke about when he laid down his life for his friends. He continued to do the right thing until the bitter end. To be that shining example of being a loving person that continues doing the right thing, no matter what.

There were at least six attempts on Jesus' life that we know about, throughout his lifetime but He did not bail out. He was born to bear witness to the truth and, he did so to the very end.

Living your life for the benefit of others instead of living for your own glory and gratification is the lesson that Jesus came to teach us.

That is true love.

Keep my commandments
Jesus said, 'As the Father has loved Me, so have I loved you. Remain in My love. If you keep My commandments, you will remain in My love, just as I have kept My Father's commandments and remain in His love. I have told you these

things so that My joy may be in you and your joy may be complete.'

Jesus said that keeping His Father's commandments kept Him in His love. And He directs us to do the same and promises us complete joy if we follow what He tells us.

Jesus loved with healing, preaching, raising people from death and providing food for the hungry. He loved by serving with humility and innocence. He kept proclaiming His Father's Word till death.

Then He said, 'Greater love does not exist than to sacrifice your life for your friends. You are my friends if you do what I command you, which is loving the way I loved you.'

He said, 'Friends, I am not writing you a new commandment, but an old one, which you have had from the very beginning. This old commandment to love each other is the same message you have heard before.'

Loving means serving
Jesus explained that loving means serving and he set the example.

He told us that the greatest among us will be the servant of all.

I guess it's similar when you consider how in families, Mum and Dad work day and night to bring up their children. Mum and Dad are in charge, but they work the hardest to serve their family.

Thanks, Mum and Dad!

Jesus told a story about a servant ploughing the field and he said that the servant would be ploughing and then serve the meal to his employer before he could sit down and eat himself.

Jesus said, "Don't expect the employer to thank the servant for doing what he's paid to do." Of course not!

The servant was simply doing his duty.

Simply doing our duty
'... when you obey me you should say, 'We are unworthy servants who have simply done our duty.'
(Luke 17:7-10)*

What Jesus was saying is that we're expected to do our duty and serve our Father as set out in His Holy Word.

Serve

For the Son of Man himself did not come to be served but to serve, and to give his life as a ransom for many.
(Mark 10:45)

Next: Chapter Ten

What Is Our Duty?

CHAPTER TEN
What is Our Duty?

How can I repay the LORD
for all His goodness to me?
I will lift the cup of salvation and
call on the name of the LORD.
(Psalm 116:12-13)

God and His Son have shown us who they are and what they will do for us if we're open to receive their love.

God, merciful, kind, and loving

God, merciful, kind, and loving, will hear us when we pray to Him and if we ask, he will save us out of all our troubles. He'll strengthen our heart and will give us peace.

Jesus will do much the same; lighten our load, give us rest and inner peace. He never gives us more than we can handle.

Jesus is also our mediator for when we muck up.

The standard is that we're told not to sin, just like Jesus. But when/if we do, we can call on Jesus, fess up, and make up, because Jesus is our advocate with our Father and the atoning sacrifice for our sins.

99

Freely you received, freely give
What are we to give in return? Both the Father and the Son give freely and we're supposed to return that favour.

Were you healed? Saved? Set free? Share!

Give freely
Freely you have received, freely give
(Matthew 10:8)

Act justly, love mercy, love the Lord and walk with Him and His Son in all you do. Serve Him with all your heart and soul.

Heal the sick, raise the dead, cleanse the lepers, drive out demons, take care of the poor and disadvantaged in society. Freely you have received; freely give.

Our whole duty is to love truly as Jesus showed us. This means serving and using our lives to help others whilst maintaining our integrity.

Truly loving means following the rules
How do we keep our integrity? We do so by sticking to the rules. The Ten that were written in stone. "*The Ten rules which are not too hard to keep.*" This quote is from Moses; God's friend. As well as from Apostle John, who was much loved by Jesus.

These rules are so simple, that any little child understands them.

Jesus said,

Unless you change course, and become as little children, you won't be invited into the kingdom of heaven. (Matthew 18:3)

These are the rules that are a given, our duty, as children of God. Following these rules is what keeps people's name safe in ones mouth. Adhering to these rules is what makes us smile and wink at each other. Following these rules is what our Father and Jesus called love.

This is what Jesus came to earth for, told us, and came to show us.

You can find my Wordpress post on this subject by typing into the Google search engine; 'God spake all these words... on love.' The URL is provided in the appendix.

Scripture tells us that we can be sure to know Jesus if we keep His Commandments. And if anyone says that they know Him, but does not keep His Commandments, he is a liar and the truth is not in him.

This makes it rather easy to detect fakes.

Jesus told all the lawless ones to stay away from him.

I've heard many people preach the gospel, but not many quote this passage from Jesus, which tells you all you need to know about doing the right thing.

By their fruits shall you recognise them

By their fruits shall you recognise them.

Not every one that says to me, Lord, Lord, shall enter into the kingdom of heaven; but he that does the will of my Father which is in heaven.

Many will say to me in that day, Lord, Lord, have we not prophesied in your name? and in your name have cast out devils? and in your name done a lot of good?

I will say, I never knew you:

go away from me,
all you who break God's laws.
(Matthew 7:20-23)

By their fruits shall you recognise them. By how they behave, their acts and their words. By how they treat you and how they make you feel. By not transgressing our Father's law.

Our Father and His Son love us for sure. But they have no reason to treat us as their own if we keep ignoring their rules.

After Jesus was crucified, his first-hand Peter assured Jesus three times in a row that he loved Him. To which Jesus responded, feed my lambs and sheep and follow me.

When we follow Jesus we're expected to walk as he walked, encourage and support one another.

Did Jesus say that just faith and believing in Him will do? Sure faith and grace come into it. God's grace is a given. Without it we are nothing.

But an appropriate response to God's grace is praise, thanks, and obedience, not complacency.

Jesus did not say that just faith and believing in Him will do.

Jesus said, just like His Father did before Him, if ye love me keep my commandments. Which Commandments? The Ten.

We're told that true love is to love without fear, and it is easy to love without fear if we follow God's guidelines, His template which spells out, in Ten easy rules how to love fearlessly.

Universal language

This is the universal language that we spoke about at the beginning of this book. The template for love that is applicable to all cultures across the world.

Who would disagree with, not lying, not killing, not stealing, not coveting, not committing adultery and so on?

This is the template that I so desperately looked for all my life. I found it in God's Holy Word; the Bible.

I'll tell you what one of the wisest men in the Bible, King Solomon, had to say about what the duty of man is:

**Fear God and
keep his commandments**
*When all has been heard,
the conclusion of the matter is this:
Fear God and keep His commandments,
for this is the whole duty of man.
(Ecclesiastes 12:13)*

I say amen to that.

Next: Chapter Eleven

God Is Love

WHAT IS TRUE LOVE? ACCORDING TO THE BIBLE

CHAPTER ELEVEN
God is Love

"Beloved, let us love one another,
for love is of God; and
everyone who loves is born of God
and knows God.
He who does not love
does not know God,
for God is love…
We love Him because
He first loved us."
(I John 4:7-8; 19)

Remember earlier when I mentioned my friends Doreen and Jim and how they make each other smile and how he winks at her at night?

That's love for you, after fifty-nine years of marriage still making each other smile and winking at each other. Smiling means joy and happiness and love.

Doreen and Jim are wonderful examples to follow and proof that it is possible to have a loving relationship after many years of marriage.

Remember that we're made in God's image and this means that we are capable of loving the way He does.

A template for loving

I've finally found my template for a truly genuine, loving relationship. Praise the Lord! And I'm ecstatic and head over heels. And this time forever after

God is love. What does that mean in my life and in the life of my children? He made me laugh when he saved us from all our troubles.

He saved me from the troubles that I created myself as well as troubles created through circumstances and other people. You can read about this in my blog post on Wordpress when you type into the Google search engine, 'Mimi says that God made her laugh.'

Love God back

God is love and we can either love God back in the way He and His Son tell us or we can love and embrace the world.

To love both at the same time is not possible. If you love the world you cannot love God and if you love God you cannot love the world. This is according to Scripture.

Saying that just faith and believing will get us there is silly.

It's not that hard to love God and His Son back.

Jesus elaborated on the kind of love that is expected from his followers and those who claim to love our Creator.

A good indication to know if you're on the right path is when you examine your feelings towards others. Do you experience love? Or hatred?

Passed from death unto life

We know that we have passed from death unto life because we love each other. He that doesn't love his brother is already dead.
(1 John 3:14)

Jesus tells us to return bad deeds with good deeds and to bless those that hate us. Turn the other cheek.

Most of us know about these sayings from Jesus. How many of us actually live like that?

This is what love is all about; continuing doing the right thing regardless of what others get up to.

As Mother Teresa said and I tell my kids all the time,

It's not between you and them, it's between you and your Father in Heaven.

Depart from evil, do good

We're told to depart from evil and do good and actively seek peace and pursue it.

What does that mean?

Well for one; don't be an idiot. Killing and destroying life is evil, and supporting life and healing is good.

If any of your friends tell you that killing others will get you to heaven; take that person straight to the emergency department in the hospital and ask for their brain to be examined.

The same goes for politicians. To think that killing others can ever be the solution for any kind of problem in the world is seriously misguided thinking.

The kind of heaven that deliberate killers expect to go to, we don't want to know about.

Actively seek a peaceful life

When a rich person asked Jesus how to get to heaven, Jesus told him to keep God's Ten Commandments.

Keeping God's Commandments means actively seeking a peaceful life.

When the person answered that he had indeed done so from his youth, Jesus told him that he should 'do good,' sell all he has and distribute amongst the poor to have treasure in heaven.

After that Jesus said, come and follow me.

However, the rich man walked away feeling sad because he was very rich.

Jesus then said that it is near impossible for rich people to enter heaven. Only with God's help will they be able to do so.

Easy message

Easy message, isn't it? Keep the Commandments, do good, and follow Jesus.

If your church/congregation isn't preaching this, they're not quoting Jesus correctly.

Churches like rich patrons because of the donations. Don't be dumbed down. Don't fool yourself either, thinking that you can buy your way into heaven.

Love God with all your heart
Loving God with all your heart and with all your understanding and with all your strength, and loving your neighbour as yourself, is way more important than all kinds of offerings and sacrifices."
(Mark 12:33)

Live a love-filled life
You may not believe in an afterlife. What about living a love-filled life now, today?

What about living on forever in the hearts of those who know you?

Stick by a few rules and be that shining example that guides those around you, lifts them up, and makes them wonder what love potion you take every morning.

Make this world a better place. Help contribute to making this world a loving place filled with smiles and respect for each other. One at a time.

Let your light shine
Let your light so shine before men, that they may see your good works, and glorify your

Father which is in heaven.
(Matthew 5:16)

Next: Chapter Twelve

God Made Me Laugh

CHAPTER TWELVE
God Made Me Laugh

Sarah said, God hath made me laugh,
so that all that hear will laugh with me.
(Genesis 21:6)

When I read the Verses about people who love their life will lose it, and those who hate their lives will keep it unto life eternal, my own life started to make sense to me for the first time ever. And once more God made me laugh! Haha, much as I tried to love all the perks of a charmed life, it just didn't do it for me.

How is it possible to love wealth and riches when there is so much unresolved poverty and suffering all around us? Guess who runs in rat races?

God's Word, however, I love with a passion, His Son; I'm head over heels. Haha, so good!

Their template for living and loving… it does not come any better.

You can decide for yourself if 'Christian loving' is different from 'mainstream loving'.

How to be saved?
How to save us from ourselves?

The message of salvation is wrapped up in the directions on how to treat and love each other.

I've looked for half a century and not found a better template on how to be truly loving than the 'The Ten.'

You can find our video on 'What is Love'? on Youtube;   https://youtu.be/hFbBERYN88o Scripture is by Moses, Jesus, and the Apostle John. Music of this video is courtesy of Art of Noise 'Moments in Love.'

What Is the Love of God?

This is the love of God

This commandment that I give you today is certainly not too difficult or not possible for you to keep. (Deuteronomy 30:11)

This is the love of God, that we keep his commandments: and his commandments are not hard to keep. (1 John 5:3)

Now you may say, 'Mimi, you keep repeating yourself.' But you know, it's not me repeating myself, it's the Holy Word, this ancient manuscript filled with age-old wisdom saying the same thing, again and again, in different ways, till we get it.

According to Scripture, we show our love for God by obeying his Commandments, and they are not that hard to follow.

What is true love (according to Scripture)?

True love in my life is *not,* as Pink says, 'hating every word that comes out of someone's mouth.' Doing the dishes comes closer. But true love according to the Bible is easy:

This is love

*That we walk according to His commandments.
This is the very commandment you have heard
from the beginning, that you must walk in love.
(2 John 1:6)*

Scripture tells us that love is being good to each other according to the directions given to us by our Creator. Quite straightforward really, a child and anyone with a sincere heart can do it.

It is pretty simple, the Commandments sum up how we are to love. Not following them is lawlessness where everyone does whatever they fancy. I cringe every time I remember the awful situations that I co-created; where everyone, including me, just made it up as we saw fit.

Our name is safe in the mouths of those who love us because loving people don't lie, kill, hate, steal, covet, and so on.

We smile at each other because we feel good, are filled with God's love and peace, and want others to feel the same.

We love fearlessly because we know that we're doing the right thing and can live without fear of repercussions now or later.

The Commandments done away with?

I've been told again and again by many Christians, friends and family, that 'the Commandments have been done away with because Jesus fulfilled them.'

Yes, Jesus did fulfil the commandments and then he said,

*"Do not think that I came to get rid of the Law or the Prophets. I did not come to discontinue the law or their wise words but
I came to show you how it is done."*
Matthew 5:17

It's a given that we keep His Commandments. They are not done away with. Our Father and His Son Jesus tell us that the Commandments are tied in with everlasting life.

Fix my words in
your hearts and minds
*Fix these words of mine in your hearts and minds,
tie them as a sign on your hands and bind them on your foreheads.
Teach them to your children.
(Deuteronomy 11:18)*

119

My law in their minds and hearts
I will put My law in their minds
and inscribe it on their hearts.
And I will be their God,
and they will be My people…
(Jeremiah 31:32-34)

I delight to do your will
"I delight to do Your will, O my God;
Your law is within my heart."
(Psalm 40:8)

As we can see below, Jesus wasn't making up His own rules; He quoted from the prophets.

Life everlasting
Jesus said that love is following God's Commandments. How do we know that Jesus spoke about God's Commandments? Because he elaborated on this, he told us just like his Father did that the Commandments are life everlasting.

Moses said,

Life everlasting
Take to heart all the words which I testify
among you this day; command your children to
observe to do, all the words of this law.
These aren't idle words I speak;

because it is your life...
([Deuteronomy 32:46-47](#))

Jesus said,

These aren't my own words, I'm telling you
what the Father, who sent me here,
commanded me to tell you and talk about.
And I know that his commandment
is life everlasting:
Whatsoever my Father told me, that is exactly
what I'm telling you.
([John 12:50](#))

A Template for Love

I love God's rules because they set a benchmark and, now I have my template to live by. A template for love. This means that my everyday life can be filled with love.

Heaven sounds beautiful, but if I were to qualify, I hope that to be far away.

I'm living now, today, and am aiming to live a love-filled life every minute of every day.

This doesn't mean that I never muck up. Not a day goes by where I don't find that I could have done better, And this is where I remember Mary, as Jesus told us to.

This is not about Jesus' mother, but a Mary who, just like us, made mistakes. She also loved much and had great faith. She simply did what she could. And we're told that because of her good work, love, and faith, her sins were forgiven her and Jesus told her to go in peace.

That means there is hope for all of us. And I reckon that is Good News, if ever I heard any.

You can listen to the song of *Mary and the Alabaster Box* on Soundcloud. The URL of

<u>Mary's story</u> throughout the Gospels is in the appendix. Lyrics are below.

Saved through good work, Love and faith

She put the ointment of spikenard, very costly.
She put it on his body for his burial.
Mary wrought a good work on Jesus.
Let her alone.
She done what she could.
Mary wrought a good work on him.
An alabaster box of very precious ointment.
She poured it on his head as he sat at meat.
She done what she could.
She wrought a good work on him.
Mary wrought a good work on Jesus.
Let her alone.
She done what she could.
Spikenard very costly.
With her hair she wiped his feet.
She did it for his burial.
It'll be told for a memorial.

Thank you, Father, for opening our eyes.

Open my eyes

Open my eyes that I may see
the wondrous things from Your law.
I am a stranger on the earth;

do not hide Your commandments from me.
(Psalm 119:18)

Next: Afterword

AFTERWORD

Behold, I set before you this day a blessing and a curse.

Why do I feel so strongly about sharing this wonderful template for living and loving?

Because I wish that I had known about God's Commandments earlier in life. Sure, I had a sense of right and wrong, but society was always arguing with me about what my conscience told me.

By the time I discovered God's Commandments I had broken each and every one of them and some many times over.

Early on in this book, I promised a shortcut on 'how-to-love-truly.'

Sticking to our Father's rules is the quickest, easiest, and most simple way to show love for each other.

Since I discovered God's wonderful rules, I've been ridiculed and mocked relentlessly because of my beliefs.

127

of faith' have called me cursed
y commitment to follow God's
ts and spreading the message.

ells us that it is the other way
around.

A blessing and a curse
*Behold, I set before you this day a blessing and
a curse;*

*A blessing, if ye obey the commandments of
the Lord your God, which I command you this
day:*

*And a curse, if ye will not obey the
commandments of the Lord your God…
(Deuteronomy 11:26-28)*

I like you to make up your own mind and not
mindlessly believe what churches and 'faithful
parishioners' tell you.

Don't believe false prophets in real life or in the
Bible. And certainly, don't believe Pharisees!

Watch out for Pharisees
*'Be careful,' Jesus said. 'Watch out for the
yeast of the Pharisees and Sadducees.'*

WHAT IS TRUE LOVE? ACCORDING TO THE BIBLE

(Matthew 16:6, see also Luke 11:37–54, Matthew 23:1–39, Mark 12:35–40, Luke 20:45–47)

Why did Jesus die?
Next time someone asks you, "Why did Jesus die?" Don't be lazy and self-centred and say, *'To save us from our sins,'* or, *'so that we may live.'*

Next time around be more truthful and say, 'Jesus was born to set an example for all of us (be a witness to the truth).

In all his doings and sayings, Jesus genuinely pointed to our Father whilst the clergy of the time and many of their followers merely paid lip service.

Jesus was crucified because His truly loving nature, His innocence and exemplary example exposed the hypocrisy of those around Him.

Tragically, this is why the Son of God died and sadly today nothing much has changed.'

Lip service
"...these people draw near to me with their mouths, and honour me with their lips, yet have removed their hearts far from me. Moreover, their worship toward me is the doctrines of men."

129

(Isaiah 29:13)

These people honour Me with their lips, but their hearts are far from Me. They worship Me in vain; they teach as doctrine the precepts of men.

(Matthew 15:8)

What does good ol' common sense tell you? Just believe, have faith, and you'll be right? Grace will rain down on you from heaven whilst you continue on your merry way? Because we're all sinners after all?

Or...

Yes, believe and have faith, thank The Lord, praise Him for His amazing grace whilst doing your part by loving each other in the way as stipulated in God's Holy Word.

Not the lukewarm love-is-kind-and-caring variety, but enthusiastically determining to follow the specific instructions as set out by Our Father and His Son.

Do your own research. It's fun and easy to do as I'll show you under the Heading, 'Resources and Examples.' Find out for yourself what the Father and His Son tell you through the Holy Spirit.

Don't rely on other people's interpretation of The Holy Word. Including mine. The Bible was written for you. Read it!

If not for my faith, I would not be alive. After a number of medical emergencies, I'm still breathing and living, whilst not many, if any (onlookers), thought that I would be. My life has miraculously turned around for the better. My children's lives have turned around for the better.

I credit our Father and His Son who sent and continues to send me wonderful helpers and keep me going against the odds.

Read '_Be Careful What You Ask For; A Horse May Grant Your Wish!_' to see how I kept ignoring nudges and despite this was saved from more serious injury.

His Word is my lifeline, His Son my forever after, and His Commandments my guiding light.

Praise the Lord YHVH and His Son Yeshua.

Pray and follow your heart.

Be kind please, Father

Be kind to your servants Lord, that we may live and obey you.
(Psalm 119:17)

May God bless your journey. I pray that my readers will enjoy a loving and peaceful life.

Mimi

Next:

God' Commandments

WHAT IS TRUE LOVE? ACCORDING TO THE BIBLE

GOD'S COMMANDMENTS

also known as 'The Ten'
Template for Love

And he gave Moses, when he finished talking with him on mount Sinai, two tables of testimony, tables of stone, written with the finger of God. (Exodus 31:18)

… Listen to all the words and close them in your hearts and command your children to do and keep all the words of this law. This is not a small thing; it is your life… (Deuteronomy 32:46-47)

I

I am God, who saved you. Only respect and admire me (what is good) and not evil. No other gods.

II

Don't create images nor likenesses of anything that is in heaven above, or in the earth beneath, nor of those things that are in the waters under the earth.
Don't admire nor serve them. You and your children and your children's children will be in trouble if you do. I will show mercy unto

thousands that love me, and keep my commandments.

III

Don't take my name in vain. You'll be punished if you do.

IV

Remember to keep one day a week holy; the Sabbath day. You'll work six days but the seventh day is the Sabbath of the Lord thy God. Don't work on that day. Not you, nor your son, nor your daughter, nor your employee or servant, nor your animals that live with you. For in six days the Lord made heaven and earth, and the sea, and all things that are in them, and rested on the seventh day: therefore the Lord blessed the seventh day, and sanctified it.

V

Honour your mum and dad;

that you may live long.

VI

Don't kill.

VII

Don't commit ʾ

VIII

Don't steal.

IX

Don't lie.

X

Don't covet.

Eternal life
I know that His commandment leads to eternal life. Therefore I tell you exactly what my Father told me to say. (John 12:50)

This is love
This commandment that I give you today is certainly not too difficult or not possible for you to keep. (Deuteronomy 30:11)

This is the love of God, that we keep his commandments: and his commandments are not hard to keep. (1 John 5:3)

gs and promises

ll known that the Commandments contain ings and promises.

e first promise is a promise of trouble for those ho violate the second Commandment.

The second promise is that mercy will be shown to those who love God and keep His Commandments.

The third promise is one of punishment for those who take God's name in their mouth for no good reason.

The seventh day of the week is designated as a rest day for God's people and Our Father blessed this day.

Then there's the promise/blessing of long life for those who honour their elders (Mum and Dad).

Earlier today I was reading Dwight L Moody's Christian's classic (available from Amazon), *How To Study The Bible.*

Dwight's book starts with a Scripture verse that I like to finish with, from Psalms.

Abundant peace

*Abundant peace have they who love Your Law;
nothing makes them stumble.
(Psalm 119:165)*

I write about this all the time because I am passionate that God's Word does not get corrupted but is truthfully presented.

Sign up here to find out when Book Three in the Truth, Love & God Series; *'The Core Message of the Bible in a few pages; The Truth About The Good News.'* will be published.

Thank you for leaving a review on Amazon if you enjoyed, *'How to Love According to God's Will? - This is Love!*

Next: Resources and Examples

Resources and Examples

I recommend that you do your own research on what the Bible has to say about 'love.' You can listen to God's Holy Word online here. (Courtesy of Bible Gateway and reader Max McLean.)

You can read the Bible in your preferred language and translation by clicking here. (Courtesy of Bible Gateway and the various publishing companies.)

To get a hard copy of the Bible you can walk into any church, where they will readily provide you with one, or you can download a Bible app here or here and read your preferred version in your favourite format.

For my research I use various Bibles and resources. Here is a link to a write-up about my best and favourite Bible resources to help you explore God's Holy Word for yourself.

You can find all the URLs referred to above in the appendix.

Examples on how to research
Don't take my word for anything but check all the Scripture verses out for yourself.

I'll give you two examples on how to easily research the Bible for yourself.

EXAMPLE ONE

We'll go to www.Biblehub.com and type in Psalm 31:19, and what comes up is this promise:

How great is your goodness

How great is Your goodness which You have laid up for those who fear You, and bestowed on those who take refuge in You in the sight of the sons of men. (Psalm 31:19)

Next, I suggest that you select 'parallel.'

This is written in blue on the top left of your screen.

Parallel

Now this verse will come up in nearly THIRTY different Bible translations. Wow! How cool is this? All verses say the same thing but use slightly different words, and this may help you to get a better understanding of what this verse means.

EXAMPLE TWO

If you're curious about what kind of goodness the promise is about, you can go to the right column of your screen and under Study Bible

Study Bible

right click on the word goodness and find the Hebrew word, word origin, phonetic spelling and definition mentioned in various popular Concordances.

Other Bible verses with the same word will be listed here as well, which will give you an even more thorough understanding of what the word goodness means in this particular context.

The above are two simple and invaluable ways you can research the meaning of Scripture for yourself. Please do!

At the moment you're reading Book Two; 'What is True Love According To The Bible?'

Next: Excerpt of Book One in the *Truth, Love & God Series.*

Excerpt from Book One

Tthe Truth, Love & God Series; 'How to Love according to God's Will? This is Love!'

In my previous book, 'How to Love according to God's Will. This is Love!' I have a conversation with my handyman on how to love according to the will of our Father.

Beginning of excerpt

"Religion is the cause of most of the wars and hatred in the world," my newfound friend Brad said.

I asked him if he really believed that and without even thinking about it, he shot back at me,

"I do not believe it, I'm convinced of it!"

"All religions?" I asked him.

Without hesitation, he responded, *"ALL of them."*

I said, *"Funny that, because my religion tells me that we are to love each other."*

"What religion would that be?" he quizzed.

"I love God's Word," I said.

3. "Mmpphh, you're one of those Christians"

"Mmpphh, you're one of those Christians," He said.

Clearly, Brad was assuming things. What was I to say to that? I did not know what he meant when he said, 'one of those,' but I wanted him to like me and not hate me because of my religion.

But more than that, I wanted to get across to him that my religion is one of love.

I was not quite sure how to go about that because Brad clearly had preconceived notions about Christianity and what it entails being a Christian or being someone that loves God's Word.

I didn't know what his preconceived ideas were, other than that they weren't positive.

4. "I Love God's Word"

So I repeated what is true for me and said, *"I love God's Word."*

Brad came over and sat down next to me.

"You mean the Bible, don't you?"

I nodded affirmatively.

Well, that really got him going. He stood up again and walked up and down my living room with the spanner in his left hand, waving his arms up and down in despair.

"The Bible has caused more wars and deaths and calamity than all other religions combined! How anyone can believe in fairy tales like that is beyond me."

End of excerpt Book One

At the moment you're reading Book Two; *'What is True Love According To The Bible?'*

Next: Excerpt of Book Three in the *Truth, Love & God Series*.

Excerpt from Book Three

Truth, Love & God Series

'The Core Message of The Bible In A Few Pages. The Truth About The Good News.'

God's Holy Word is About Love

The core message of the Bible is about love.

Early in the Bible, we are provided with Love Rules.

Within the pages of this phenomenal bestseller-of-all-time, we discover who God is and what the truth is about, 'true love.'

Google and Oxford dictionaries tell us that God is the Creator and Ruler of the universe and source of all moral authority; the supreme being.'

We'll find out more about Him later.

Myriad examples are given throughout history on how our Heavenly Father wants us to love Him back, and how we fail to stick to the rules.

We don't fail to stick to the rules because we're not able to. Our Father would not ask us for something we are not capable of. His rules are easy. We don't obey because we cannot be bothered. Just like Adam and Eve. How hard is it to not touch what isn't yours?

Throughout the Bible, we're told what the consequences of our shortcomings are.

The foreword by King Nebuchadnezzar tells us that God is in charge.

The beauty of this is that as long as we follow the guidelines and do our best, we can relax and leave the rest to God.

When we decide to heed the warnings, what becomes clear early in the Bible is that we're rewarded, blessed for Godly behaviour, and penalties apply for beastly behaviour.

There is a warning in God's Holy Word for all of us to:

Listen and understand
Everyone that lives on this earth shall worship The Beast, everyone whose name has not been written in
THE BOOK OF LIFE,
If you have ears, listen and understand!
Revelation 13:7-15

This book, '*The Core Message of the Bible in a Few Pages; The Truth About The Good News*' is for anyone who wants to know if their name has been written in THE BOOK OF LIFE, and if not, why not. If this is you, read on.

A quick Google search tells me that in Christianity and Judaism, the Book of Life (Hebrew: ספר החיים, transliterated Sefer HaChaim; Greek: βιβλίον τῆς ζωῆς Biblíon tēs Zōēs) is the book in which God records the names of every person who is destined for Heaven or the World to Come.

Blessings and good stuff
To find out if the blessings and all the good stuff that some people take for granted in their life are available to you also, read on.

Blessings and good stuff
A blessing on your goods and everything to which you put your hand; The LORD will establish you as His special people, just as He has sworn to you if you keep the commandments of the LORD your God and walk in His ways. Deuteronomy 28:8-9

Sounds easy, doesn't it? Keep his Commandments, walk in His ways, and you'll be blessed. Is this what the churches and synagogues teach us? Not quite. Read on to see what else the Bible has to say about God's love and his blessings.

Summation of the Bible
This short book is a summation of the history book of the Jewish people. Also known as The Bible, The Word of God, and The Truth.

'The Core Message of the Bible in a few pages; 'The Truth About The Good News' explains how God defines love and how to stay on the right side of our Father. We'll go through the Bible quick smart to learn from others' mistakes.

We'll learn that God loves us and how He wants us to love Him back.

Is the Bible fact or fiction?
I have family members who think that the Bible is a fairy tale. In my own life, the Bible is the only truth. However, you can read this book as fact or fiction; it doesn't matter. Just see if it makes sense to you either way.

I've lived with beasts and have been beastly myself. I'm done with it.

Life has been no fairytale to me. At some stages, it sucked BIG TIME! Until I came across God's

Love Rules and found this wonderful standard to live by.

Rules on How to Love Each Other. Yes!
The moment I found these rules I became ecstatically happy. So enamoured, in fact, that I copied these rules and sent them to all my friends and family members.

As in, 'Hey, did you know, there are rules to live by? How wonderful. There is a God and He set a standard for us to live by; moral guidelines. WOW!'

I was over the moon. No more bullying or strategising. Just follow these simple rules to live a blessed, respectful, and balanced life. Yeah!!

Needless to say, none of my friends nor family responded to my enthusiastic invitation to follow some basic rules.

The religious ones kicked me out altogether because of my ignorance. If you're part of God's family, you don't have to follow His guidelines, I was told. You're made holy, just by believing. Righto. Sounds brilliant. But is it true? I wasn't sure, so I kept reading.

My non-believing friends were slightly bemused by my enthusiasm, but other than that didn't really give it too much attention.

Chapter One

Bible application lessons

God is the Creator and Ruler of our universe. His Holy Word tells us how to love truly. When you're tempted to do the wrong or beastly thing, turn to the Father and His Son, who are our perfect examples, for help. And you'll find that the temptation will disappear. Remember that the kingdom of God is within you.

You'll be blessed if you follow the directions of our Heavenly Father and His Son and live accordingly.

Blessed are those who follow God's law.
Psalm 1:1-2

End of Excerpt

Next: Scripture References for

'What Is True Love According To The Bible?'

Scripture References

What Is True Love According to the Bible?

https://mailchi.mp/335790139737/tlg2ref

DEDICATION REFERENCES

Teach our children
Remember my words in your heart and your soul… and teach them to your children. (Deuteronomy 11:18-21)

MANY THANKS

Prophetesses Huldah, Sarah, Miriam, Deborah, Hannah, Abigail, and Esther and Anna.

INTRODUCTION REFERENCES

God is love
Anyone who doesn't love does not know

God, because God is love. (1 John 4:8)

Love others as yourself
Love others as you love yourself…
(Leviticus 19:18, Matthew 19:19)

Making it up as we go along
In those days there was no king in Israel: every man did that which was right in his own eyes. (Judges 21:25)

In those days Israel had no king; everyone did as they saw fit. (Judges 17:6)

There is no fear in love

There is no fear in love. True love for others is fearless. If the thought of repercussions scares us, this means that we have not really learned to love. (1 John 4:18)

Love your neighbour as yourself
Love your neighbour as yourself…
(Leviticus 19:18, Matthew 19:19)

HOW TO READ THIS BOOK

Gutenberg printing press
https://en.wikipedia.org/wiki/Gutenberg_Bible

Bible Gateway Audio
https://www.biblegateway.com/passage/?search=genesis+1&version=KJV

Bible Gateway Bibles in various translations
https://www.biblegateway.com/versions/

https://www.bible.com/app

Bible apps for your computer/tablet or laptop
https://www.youversion.com/the-bible-app/

My 15 best Biblical resources
https://liveforeverhowto.wordpress.com/2016/05/06/15-of-my-best-and-favourite-biblical-resources/

EXAMPLE ONE
www.biblehub.com type in Psalm 31:19 and parallel
https://biblehub.com/psalms/31-19.htm

How great is your goodness

How great is Your goodness which You have laid up for those who fear You, and bestowed on those who take refuge in You in the sight of the sons of men. (Psalm 31:19)

EXAMPLE TWO
Right-click on the word goodness:
https://biblehub.com/hebrew/2898.htm

You can download the Scriptural references for 'What is True Love According to the Bible?" here.

https://mailchi.mp/335790139737/tlg2ref

The Book of Truth
I will tell you what is written in The Book of Truth. (Daniel 10:21)

CHAPTER ONE REFERENCES

Loved in spite of ourselves
"The greatest happiness of life is the conviction that we are loved; loved for ourselves, or rather, loved in spite of ourselves." Victor Hugo

Jesus also commanded that we love each other
And now I give you a new commandment: love one another. As I have loved you, so you must love one another. (John 13:34)

Don't hate
Whoever hates his brother is a murderer: and you know that no murderer will live forever. (1 John 3:15)

Have a good heart

Those things which fall out of our mouth come from the heart; and they degrade and tarnish us.

It's from the heart that we get evil thoughts, murders, adulteries, fornications, thefts, false witness, blasphemies... (Matthew 15:18-19)

Don't call each other names

If you're angry with your brother without any reason, you'll be in danger of divine judgment: and whosoever says to his brother, idiot, is risking a tribunal hearing: but whosoever says, you fool, risks being thrown in hell. (Matthew 5:21-23)

Control your tongue

Most of us get it wrong quite often. Try finding someone who never offends anyone and you've found the perfect person who can control his/her whole body.

We put bits in horses' mouths so that they obey us, and with this bit we can turn their whole body. Same with ships: large as they may be, and facing the strongest possible winds, they are perfectly managed by the captain steering the small helm.

Even so, the tongue is tiny in comparison to the body, and yet it can create massive mayhem and start massive fires.

The tongue is a fire, potentially filled with bad stuff. And the tongue is part of our body that can taint everything else about us and ruin everything to the point of us ending up in hell because of it.

160

You can tame all kinds of beasts, and birds, and serpents, and all kinds of living creatures in the sea are tamed by mankind:

But no one has yet tamed their tongue; it is an unruly evil, full of deadly poison.

With it we bless God, our Father; and with it we curse men, who are made after the likeness of God.

Out of the same mouth we hear blessings and cursing. This should not be. Control your tongue!

(James 3:1-10)

Steer the traffic of our words.
'Steer the traffic of our words,' as mentioned in *Power up Your Self-talk: 6 Simple Habits to Stop Beating Yourself Up and Reclaim Your Life*' by Michal Stawicki. Available from Amazon.

A loving God
A merciful and gracious God, endlessly patient, abundant in lovingkindness and truth, lavishing unfailing love to generations, forgiving sin and holding the guilty accountable. (Exodus 34:6-7)

We're made in God's image
God created man in his own image, in the image of God created he him; male and female created He them. (Genesis 1:27)

Don't speak idle words

But I say unto you, That every idle word that you shall speak, you shall have to give account of this on the day of judgment.

(Matthew 12:36)

CHAPTER TWO REFERENCES

We are commanded to love each other
I command you to love one another.
(John 15:17)

Love one another
... love one another; as I have loved you... also love one another.

By this shall all men know that ye are my disciples, if ye have love one to another. (John 13:34-35)

From the beginning... love each other
The message you heard from the very beginning is this: we must love one another. (1 John 3:11)

Love your neighbour
Thou shalt not avenge, nor bear any grudge against the children of thy people, but thou shalt love thy neighbour as thyself: I am the Lord. (Leviticus 19:18)

Love the foreigner
The foreigner that lives with you shall be unto you as one born among you, and you shall love him as yourself... (Leviticus 19:34)

The message from the beginning

The message you heard from the very beginning is this: we must love one another. (1 John 3:11)

CHAPTER THREE REFERENCES

Lay down your life

Greater love hath no man than this, that a man lay down his life for his friends. (John 15:13)

Sweat like blood

And being in an agony he prayed more earnestly: and his sweat was as it were great drops of blood falling down to the ground. (Luke 22:44)

What does it mean if you sweat blood?

Hematidrosis is a condition in which capillary blood vessels that feed the sweat glands rupture, causing them to exude blood. This phenomenon is known to occur under conditions of extreme physical or emotional stress.

Your will be done

... A second time He went away and prayed, "My Father, if this cup cannot pass unless I drink it, may Your will be done..." (Matthew 26:36-45)

He is innocent

When Pilate saw that he could prevail nothing, but that rather a tumult was made, he took water, and washed his hands before the multitude, saying, I am innocent of the blood of this just person: see ye to it. (Matthew 27:24)

Bearing witness to the truth

"You say that I am a king. To this end was I born, and for this cause came I into the world, that I should bear witness unto the truth. Every one that is of the truth heareth my voice." (John 18:37)

Scripture of Truth
But I will show you what is written in the scripture of truth… (Daniel 10:21)

Sanctify them through your truth: your word is truth. (John 17:17)

The Word was made flesh
And the Word was made flesh, and dwelt among us, (and we beheld his glory, the glory of the only begotten of the Father,) full of grace and truth. (John 1:14, 18)

Jesus - Yeshua - Saviour
The name Jesus (IPA: /ˈdʒiːzəs/) is derived from the name Iēsous (Greek: Ἰησοῦς), the Greek form of the Hebrew name Yeshua (Hebrew: ישוע). As its roots lie in the name Yeshua, it is etymologically related to another biblical name, Joshua.

The Hebrew Bible uses Yehoshua (יְהוֹשֻׁעַ) for Joshua, which means "Yah is Salvation." Many nowadays reject the term Yahshua (יהשע) in favor of Yeshua (ישוע) as the original pronunciation.

Save people from their sins.
And she shall give birth to a son, and you shall call his name YESHUA (Jesus): for he shall save his people from their sins. (Matthew 1:21)

Sin is lawlessness

Everyone who practices sin practises lawlessness as well. Indeed, sin is lawlessness... in Jesus there is no sin... (1 John 3:4)

All wrongdoing is called sin... (1 John 5:17)

If you sin you're of the devil
Those who keep sinning are of the devil, because the devil has been sinning from the beginning. The reason the Son of God appeared was to destroy the devil's work. (1 John 3:8)

Save people from their sins
And she shall give birth to a son, and you shall call his name YESHUA (Jesus): for he shall save his people from their sins. (Matthew 1:21)

CHAPTER FOUR REFERENCES

No fault in him... just person
Pilate said... I find in him no fault at all.

I find no fault in him... I find no fault in him... The King of the Jews... I am innocent of the blood of this just person... (John 17:38, John 19:4-6, Matthew 27:24)

Hypocrisy
Even so ye also outwardly appear righteous unto men, but within ye are full of hypocrisy and iniquity. (Matthew 23:28)

Then spake Jesus to the multitude, and to his disciples, Saying The scribes and the Pharisees sit in Moses' seat: All therefore whatsoever they bid you observe, that observe and do; but do not ye after their works: for they say, and do not… (Matthew 23)

… he began to say unto his disciples first of all, Beware ye of the leaven of the Pharisees, which is hypocrisy. (Luke 12:1)

No cloak for their sin
If I had not come and spoken unto them, they had not had sin: but now they have no cloak for their sin. (John 15:22)

Evil deeds
And this is the condemnation, that light is come into the world, and men loved darkness rather than light, because their deeds were evil. (John 3:19)

God gave His Son
God gave his only begotten son. For God so loved the world that He gave His one and only Son, that everyone who believes in Him shall not perish but have eternal life. For God did not send His Son into the world to condemn the world, but to save the world through Him… (John 3:1-17)

Jesus' life a ransom for many
'For the Son of Man himself did not come to be served but to serve, and to give his life as a ransom for many'. (Mark 10:45)

Born to bear witness to the truth
"For this reason I was born and have come into the world, to testify to the truth. Everyone who belongs to the truth listens to My voice." (John 18:36-38)

Forgiveness of sins

'Drink all of you from this', he said. 'For this is my blood, the blood of the covenant, which is to be poured out for many for the forgiveness of sins.' (Matthew 26:28)

Jesus is the resurrection and the life

Jesus said to her, "I am the resurrection and the life. He who believes in Me will live, even though he dies. (John 11:25)

Children of God

Behold what manner of love the Father has given to us, that we should be called children of God. And that is what we are! The reason the world does not know us is that it did not know Him. (1 John 3:1)

God sent His Son

This is how God's love was revealed among us: God sent His one and only Son into the world, so that we might live through Him. (1 John 4:9)

Why do you hate me so much?

Many good works did I show you from my Father; for which of those works do you stone me? (John 19:32)

TRUE LOVE

God's love

This is how God's love was revealed among us; that He sent His one and only Son into the world so that we might live through Him. (1 John 4:9)

True love

This is true love; not that we loved God, but that he loved us and sent his Son as a sacrifice to take away our sins. (1 John 4:10)

The Lamb of God
'... Look, the Lamb of God,
which takes away the sin of the world.' (John 1:29, 1 John 3:5)

God hears people who do his will
Now we know that God doesn't hear sinners: but if anyone worships God, and does his will, He'll hear him. (John 9:31)

God hears and helps good people
When good people cry, God hears them and delivers them out of all their troubles. (Psalm 34:17)

Sinners break God's Law
People who sin break God's Law. Sin is lawlessness, (1 John 3:4)

In Him there is no sin
You know that Christ appeared to take away sins, and in Him there is no sin. No one who remains in Him keeps on sinning. No one who continues to sin has seen Him or known Him. (1 John 3:5-6)

No cover for their sin
If I had not come and spoken unto them, they had not had sin: but now they have no cover for their sin. (John 15:22)

CHAPTER FIVE REFERENCES

Repent or perish

There were present at that season some that told him of the Galileans whose blood Pilate had mingled with their sacrifices.

And Jesus answering said unto them, Suppose ye that these Galileans were sinners above all the Galileans, because they suffered such things?

I tell you, Nay: but, except ye repent, ye shall all likewise perish.

Or those eighteen, upon whom the tower in Siloam fell, and slew them, think ye that they were sinners above all men that dwelt in Jerusalem?

I tell you, Nay: but, except ye repent, ye shall all likewise perish. (Luke 13:1-5)

Bear fruit or be cut down

He spake this parable; A certain man had a fig tree planted in his vineyard; and he came and sought fruit thereon, and found none.

Then said he unto the dresser of his vineyard, Behold, these three years I come seeking fruit on this fig tree, and find none: cut it down; why cumbereth it the ground?

And he answering said unto him, Lord, let it alone this year also, till I shall dig about it, and dung it:

And if it bear fruit, well: and if not, then after that thou shalt cut it down. (Luke 13:6-9)

Punishment according to your deeds

...I will punish you according to the fruit of your deeds, said the LORD… (Jeremiah 21:14)

Example One - Do not swear
You shall not take the name of the Lord God (YHVH) in vain; for you'll be in trouble if you do. (Exodus 20:7)

Example Two - Do not steal
You shall not steal. (Exodus 20:15)

Example Three - Do not lie - honour your parents
Honour your father and mother: so that you may live long upon the land which the Lord God gives you. (Exodus 20:12)

Example Four - Do not commit adultery
You shall not commit adultery. (Exodus 20:14)

Example Five - Do not covet
You shall not covet your neighbour's house, wife, nor his servant, nor his ox, nor his ass, nor anything that belongs to you neighbour. (Exodus 20:17)

Example Six - Honour God only
You shall have no other gods before me. (Exodus 20:3)

Church doctrine as opposed to God's Holy Word

Part one
https://liveforeverhowto.wordpress.com/2014/07/18/a-message-from-jesus-about-churches-part-one-2/

Part two
https://liveforeverhowto.wordpress.com/2014/07/22/leap-for-joy-a-message-from-jesus-about-churches-part-two/

God's Feasts
Our Father tells us what kind of Feasts he likes us to celebrate in the Book of Leviticus 23. He calls them HIS Feasts.

Heresy
Heresy (/ˈhɛrəsi/) is any belief or theory that is strongly at variance with established beliefs or customs, in particular the accepted beliefs of a church or religious organization. https://en.wikipedia.org/wiki/Heresy

In vain they worship me - commandments of men
But in vain they do worship me, teaching for doctrines the commandments of men. (Matthew 15:9)

Forgotten my law
My people are destroyed for lack of knowledge. Because you have rejected knowledge, I will also reject you as My priests. Since you have forgotten the law of your God, I will also forget your children. (Hosea 4:6)

Religious leaders are often distrusted

In 2019, according to ABC's Australia Talks National Survey, religious leaders were distrusted by a full 70 per cent of the population, with 35 percent saying they did not trust them "at all." And even within their own flocks, religious leaders were viewed with some suspicion.

https://www.abc.net.au/news/2019-11-06/annabel-crabb-australia-talks-religion-insights/11674076   and also https://australiatalks.abc.net.au/

CHAPTER SIX REFERENCES

Duty of the priest

The duty of the priest is to teach knowledge of good and evil but you have lost your way and caused many to stumble into sin... you have violated the covenant... (Malachi 2:7-9)

Laying aside the commandment of God

For laying aside the commandment of God, ye hold the tradition of men, as the washing of pots and cups: and many other such like things ye do. (Mark 7:8)

If we claim we have not sinned, we make Him out to be a liar and His word is not in us. (1 John 1:10)

We are his flock

"Son of man, prophesy against the shepherds of Israel. Prophecy and tell them that this is what the Lord GOD says: 'Woe to the shepherds of Israel, who only feed themselves! Should not the shepherds feed their flock? (Ezekiel 34:2)

"Woe to the shepherds who destroy and scatter the sheep of My pasture!" declares the LORD. (Jeremiah 23:1)

Apostle John agrees that we're all sinners

If we say that we have no sin, we deceive ourselves, and the truth is not in us.

If we confess our sins, he is faithful and just to forgive us our sins, and to cleanse us from all unrighteousness.

If we say that we have not sinned, we make him a liar, and his word is not in us. (1 John 1:8-10)

Walk as He walked
He that saith he abideth in him ought himself also so to walk, even as he walked. (1 John 2:6)

Abraham was blessed because he obeyed
And I will make thy seed to multiply as the stars of heaven, and will give unto thy seed all these countries; and in thy seed shall all the nations of the earth be blessed;

Because that Abraham obeyed my voice, and kept my charge, my commandments, my statutes, and my laws. (Genesis 26:4-6)

Noah was just and perfect
These are the generations of Noah: Noah was a just man and perfect in his generations, and Noah walked with God. (Genesis 6:9)

Millions died but Caleb and Joshua were saved
For the Lord had said of them, They shall surely die in the wilderness. And there was not a man left of them, save Caleb the son of Jephunneh, and Joshua the son of Nun... for they have wholly followed the Lord. (Numbers 26:65, 32:12)

Both righteous... blameless
And they were both righteous before God, walking in all the commandments and ordinances of the Lord blameless. (Luke 1:6)

I did not come to heal the good people

... Jesus said, "It is not the healthy who need a doctor, but the sick. But go ye and learn what that meaneth, I will have mercy, and not sacrifice: for I am not come to call the righteous, but sinners to repentance. (Matthew 9:13)

Jesus came to call sinners to repent
On hearing this, Jesus told them, "It is not the healthy who need a doctor, but the sick. I have not come to call the righteous, but sinners." (Mark 2:17)

Jesus answered, "It is not the healthy who need a doctor, but the sick. (Luke 5:31)

"I have not come to call the righteous, but sinners to repentance." (Luke 5:32)

I say unto you, that likewise joy shall be in heaven over one sinner that repenteth, more than over ninety and nine just persons, which need no repentance. (Luke 15:7)

Sin no more
Afterward Jesus found him in the temple, and said, You've been made whole: sin no more, lest a worse thing come unto thee. (John 5:14)

She said, No man, Lord. And Jesus said unto her, Neither do I condemn thee: go, and sin no more. (John 8:11)

More joy over one sinner than ninety nine good people
In the same way, I tell you that there will be more joy in heaven over one sinner who repents than over ninety-

nine righteous ones who do not need to repent. (Luke 15:7)

Collect the weeds at harvest time
…'No,' he said, 'if you pull the weeds now, you might uproot the wheat with them. Let both grow together until the harvest. At the proper time I will tell the harvesters, "First collect the weeds and tie them in bundles to be burned; then gather the wheat into my barn." (Matthew 30:29-32)

His winnowing fork is in His hand to clear His threshing floor and to gather His wheat into the barn; but He will burn up the chaff with unquenchable fire." (Matthew 3:12)

Parable of the seeds and weeds
Then Jesus sent the multitude away, and went into the house: and his disciples came unto him, saying, Declare unto us the parable of the tares of the field.

He answered and said unto them, He that soweth the good seed is the Son of man; The field is the world; the good seed are the children of the kingdom; but the tares are the children of the wicked one; The enemy that sowed them is the devil; the harvest is the end of the world; and the reapers are the angels.

As therefore the tares are gathered and burned in the fire; so shall it be in the end of this world.

The Son of man shall send forth his angels, and they shall gather out of his kingdom all things that offend, and them which do iniquity; And shall cast them into a furnace of fire: there shall be wailing and gnashing of teeth.

Then shall the righteous shine forth as the sun in the kingdom of their Father. Who hath ears to hear, let him hear. (Matthew 13:36-43)

Seed bearing much fruit
Jesus spake unto his listeners in parables, saying, Behold, a sower went forth to sow;

And when he sowed, some seeds fell by the wayside, and the fowls came and ate all seeds:

Some fell on rocks, where they had not much earth: and forthwith they sprung up, because there was no earth:

Yet when the sun got up, they were scorched; and because they had no root, they withered away.

Some seeds fell among thorns; and the thorns sprung up, and choked them:

Other seeds fell into good ground, and brought forth fruit, some an hundredfold, some sixtyfold, some thirtyfold.

Listen up!

The disciples came, and said, why do you talk to them in parables?

He answered, Because it is given unto you to know the mysteries of the kingdom of heaven, but to them it is not given.

Whosoever hath, to him shall be given, and he shall have more abundance: but whosoever hath not, from him shall be taken away even that he hath.

I speak to them in parables: because they seeing see not; and hearing they hear not, neither do they understand.

In them is fulfilled the prophecy of Esaias, which says, By hearing ye shall hear, and shall not understand; and seeing ye shall see, and shall not perceive:

These people have hard hearts, and their ears are dull, and their eyes they have closed; in case at any time they should see with their eyes and hear with their ears, and should understand with their heart, and should be converted, and I should heal them.

But blessed are your eyes, for they see: and your ears, for they hear.

For verily I say unto you, That many prophets and righteous men have very much wanted to see those things which ye see, and have not seen them; and to hear those things which ye hear, and have not heard them.

Listen to the parable of the sower.

When anyone hears the word of the kingdom, and doesn't understand it, then comes the wicked one, and steals that which was sown in his heart. This is he which received seed by the wayside.

But he that received the seed into stony places, is the one that hears the word, and quickly with joy receives it;

However he is not stable and only lasts for a little while: as soon as he experiences trouble or persecution because of the word, he will bail.

He also that received seed among the thorns is he that hears the word; and the care of this world, and the deceitfulness of riches, choke the word, and he becomes unfruitful.

But he that received seed into the good ground is he that hears the word, and understands it; it will bear fruit, and bring forth, some an hundredfold, some sixty, some thirty.

(Matthew 13:1-23, Mark 4:1-20, Luke 8:4-15)

Separating the sheep from the goats
When the Son of man shall come in his glory, and all the holy angels with him, then shall he sit upon the throne of his glory:

And before him shall be gathered all nations: and he shall separate them one from another, as a shepherd divideth his sheep from the goats:

And he shall set the sheep on his right hand, but the goats on the left.

Then shall the King say unto them on his right hand, Come, ye blessed of my Father, inherit the kingdom prepared for you from the foundation of the world:

For I was hungry, and you gave me meat: I was thirsty, and you gave me drink: I was a stranger, and you took me in:

Naked, and you gave me clothes: I was sick, and you took care of me: I was in prison, and you visited me.

Then shall the righteous answer him, saying, Lord, when did we see you hungry, and fed you? or thirsty, and gave you something to drink?

When did we mistake you for a stranger, and took thee in? or naked, and gave you clothes?

Or when did we see you sick, or in prison, and helped and visited you?

And the King shall answer and say unto them, Verily I say unto you, Inasmuch as ye have done it unto one of the least of these my brethren, ye have done it unto me.

Then shall he say also unto them on the left hand, Depart from me, ye cursed, into everlasting fire, prepared for the devil and his angels:

For I was hungry, and you gave me no meat: I was thirsty, and you gave me no drink:

I was a stranger, and you took me not in: naked, and you clothed me not: sick, and in prison, and you visited me not.

Then shall they also answer him, saying, Lord, when did we see you hungry, or thirsty, or a stranger, or naked, or sick, or in prison, and did not help or visit you?

Then shall he answer them, saying, Verily I say unto you, Inasmuch as ye did it not to one of the least of these, ye did it not to me.

And these shall go away into everlasting punishment: but the righteous into life eternal. (Matthew 25:31-46)

How to be a good loving person
A certain lawyer stood up, and tempted him, saying, Master, what shall I do to inherit eternal life?

He said unto him, What is written in the law? how readest thou?

And he answering said, Thou shalt love the Lord thy God with all thy heart, and with all thy soul, and with all thy strength, and with all thy mind; and thy neighbour as thyself.

And he said unto him, Thou hast answered right: this do, and thou shalt live.

But he, willing to justify himself, said unto Jesus, And who is my neighbour?

Samaritan story
And Jesus answering said, A certain man went down from Jerusalem to Jericho, and fell among thieves, which stripped him of his raiment, and wounded him, and departed, leaving him half dead.

And by chance there came down a certain priest that way: and when he saw him, he passed by on the other side.

And likewise a Levite, when he was at the place, came and looked on him, and passed by on the other side.

But a certain Samaritan, as he journeyed, came where he was: and when he saw him, he had compassion on him,

And went to him, and bound up his wounds, pouring in oil and wine, and set him on his own beast, and brought him to an inn, and took care of him.

And on the morrow when he departed, he took out two pence, and gave them to the host, and said unto him, Take care of him; and whatsoever thou spendest more, when I come again, I will repay thee.

Which of these three, thinkest thou, was neighbour unto him that fell among thieves?

And he said, He that shewed mercy on him. Then said Jesus unto him, Go, and do thou likewise. (Luke 10:26-37)

Be perfect
Be perfect, therefore, as your Heavenly Father is perfect. (Matthew 5:48)

Be holy
"Speak to the entire congregation of the Israelites and tell them: 'Be holy because I, the LORD your God, am holy.'" (Leviticus 19:2)

Stop sinning
You know that Christ came to take away sins, and in Him there is no sin. No one who lives in union with Him

keeps on sinning. Everyone who continues to sin has not seen Him or known Him. (1 John 3:5-6)

Teach newcomers properly
"Woe to you, teachers of the law and Pharisees, you hypocrites! You do your utmost to win a single convert, and when you have succeeded, you make them twice as much a child of hell as you are." (Matthew 23:15)

Ask for help

The Lord heard me and saved me
I prayed to the Lord and He heard me and saved me out of all my troubles.
(Psalm 34:6)

I will give you rest
Come to me when you're tired and bent over, under the weight of your problems. I will give you rest.

Do what I tell you and learn from me. I am kind, patient and modest. I'll help you find inner peace.

What I'll tell you to do will be easy and not too hard or difficult for you. Matthew (11:28-30)

CHAPTER SEVEN REFERENCES

The verdict
This is the verdict: The Light has come into the world, but men loved the darkness rather than the Light, because their deeds were evil. (John 3:19)

Remember me according to your love

Don't remember the sins of my youth, nor my disobedience: according to your love and mercy remember me please, O LORD. (Psalm 25:7)

Will just faith do the trick?
What doth it profit, my brethren, though a man say he hath faith, and have not works? can faith save him? (James 2:14. Also read James 1, 2 and 3)

Don't remember my sins please
Don't remember the sins of my youth, nor my disobedience: according to your love and mercy remember me please, O LORD. (Psalm 25:7)

Blessings for doers - follow God's perfect law
If you look closely into the perfect law that sets people free, and keep on paying attention to it and do not simply listen and then forget it, but put it into practice; you will be blessed by God in what you do. (James 1:22-25)

Proudly acknowledge the Son of God
Whoever will be ashamed of me and of my words, of him will the Son of Man be ashamed, when he comes in his glory, and the glory of the Father, and of the holy angels. (Luke 9:26)

"Everyone who acknowledges me before men, the Son of Man will also acknowledge before the angels of God;

but he who denies me in the presence of men will be denied in the presence of God's angels." (Luke 12:8-9)

Stick together through thick and thin

183

Read the story of Ruth in the Bible.

The story of Ruth and Naomi is a heartwarming story of two women who stuck together through thick and thin and came out pretty good. Ruth turned out to be one of Jesus' ancestors. Ruth said to Naomi,

Where you go I will go

"Don't ask me to leave you. Where you go, I will go and where you sleep, I will sleep. Your people are my people and your God is my God... I pray that only death will be able to separate us." (Ruth 1:16-18)

Boaz married Ruth and she gave birth to a son.

The women said to Naomi, "Blessed be the Lord, who has not left you this day without someone to take care of you; and may his name be famous in Israel! And may he be to you a restorer of life and a nourisher of your old age; for your daughter-in-law, who loves you, who is better to you than seven sons, has borne him." Then Naomi took the child and laid him on her bosom, and became a nurse to him. Also the neighbor women gave him a name, saying, "There is a son born to Naomi." And they called his name Obed. He is the father of Jesse, the father of King David. (Ruth 4:13-17)

Sell one's soul

For what is a man profited, if he shall gain the whole world, and lose his own soul? or what shall a man give in exchange for his soul? (Matthew 16:26)

For what shall it profit a man, if he shall gain the whole world, and lose his own soul? (Mark 8:36)

CHAPTER EIGHT REFERENCES

Those who practice the truth come into the light.
Everyone who does evil hates the Light, and does not come into the Light for fear that his deeds will be exposed. But whoever practices the truth comes into the Light… (John 3:20-21)

Jesus healed them all
And everyone wanted to touch Him, for power went out from Him and healed them all. (Luke 6:19)

Do not fear for your life… Fear The Lord
I tell you, My friends, do not be afraid of those who kill the body and after that can do no more. But I will show you whom you should fear: Fear the One who, after you have been killed, has power to throw you into hell. Yes, I tell you, fear Him! (Luke 12:4-5)

Love your life and lose it
"Anyone who loves their life will lose it, while anyone who hates their life in this world will keep it for eternal life." (John 12:25)

Hatred won't get you anywhere
Thou shalt not hate thy brother in thine heart: thou shalt in any wise rebuke thy neighbour, and not suffer sin upon him. (Leviticus 19:17)

But he that hateth his brother is in darkness, and walketh in darkness, and knoweth not whither he goeth, because that darkness hath blinded his eyes. (1 John 2:11)

185

If a man says, I love God, and hates his brother, he is a liar: for he that loveth not his brother whom he hath seen, how can he love God whom he hath not seen? (1 John 4:20)

Whoever is angry with his brother without a cause shall be in danger of the judgment: and whosoever shall say to his brother, idiot, shall be in danger of the council: but whosoever shall say, Thou fool, shall be in danger of hell fire. (Matthew 5:22)

Jesus had no house
And Jesus saith unto him, The foxes have holes, and the birds of the air have nests; but the Son of man has nowhere to lay his head. (Matthew 8:20)

Jesus owned one outfit
When they had crucified Him, they divided up His garments by casting lots. (Matthew 27:35)

Share
John replied, "Whoever has two tunics should share with him who has none, and whoever has food should do the same." (Luke 3:11)

FeedtheHungry
Feed The Hungry is one of my favourite organisations where a mere $30 feeds five children for a whole month!
https://feedthehungry.org.au/give/donate

Do not love the world
Do not love the world nor the things in the world. If anyone loves the world, the love of the Father is not in

him. For all that is in the world, the lust of the flesh and the lust of the eyes and the boastful pride of life, is not from the Father, but is from the world. The world is passing away, and also its lusts; but the one who does the will of God lives forever. (1 John 2:15-17)

CHAPTER NINE REFERENCES

God gave His one and only Son

God so loved the world that He gave His one and only Son, that everyone who believes in Him shall not perish but have eternal life. For God did not send His Son into the world to condemn the world, but to save the world through Him... (John 3:1-17)

Keep My Commandments to remain in my love

As the Father has loved Me, so have I loved you. Remain in My love. If you keep My commandments, you will remain in My love, just as I have kept My Father's commandments and remain in His love. I have told you these things so that My joy may be in you and your joy may be complete. (John 15:9-11)

Love the way I loved you

This is My commandment, that you love one another as I have loved you. Greater love has no one than this, that he lay down his life for his friends. You are My friends if you do what I command you. (John 15:12-14)

Not a new commandment

Beloved, I am not writing you a new commandment, but an old one, which you have had from the beginning. This old commandment - to love each other - is the message you have heard from the beginning. (1 John 2:7-8)

We're called to serve
And Jesus called them to him and said to them, "You know that those who are considered rulers of the Gentiles lord it over them, and their great ones exercise authority over them. But it shall not be so among you. But whoever would be great among you must be your servant, and whoever would be first among you must be slave of all. For even the Son of Man came not to be served but to serve, and to give his life as a ransom for many." (Mark 10:42-45)

Let the greatest among you become as the youngest, and the leader as one who serves. For who is the greater, one who reclines at table or one who serves? Is it not the one who reclines at table? But I am among you as the one who serves. (Luke 22:26-27)

The greatest among you shall be your servant. (Matthew 23:11)

If anyone serves me, he must follow me; and where I am, there will my servant be also. If anyone serves me, the Father will honor him. (John 12:26)

And he sat down and called the twelve. And he said to them, "If anyone would be first, he must be last of all and servant of all." (Mark 9:35)

The Son of Man came not to be served but to serve, and to give his life as a ransom for many." (Matthew 20:28)

Now before the Feast of the Passover, when Jesus knew that his hour had come to depart out of this world to the Father, having loved his own who were in the world, he loved them to the end. During supper, when the devil had already put it into the heart of Judas Iscariot, Simon's son, to betray him, Jesus, knowing that the Father had given all things into his hands, and that he had come from God and was going back to God, rose from supper. He laid aside his outer garments, and taking a towel, tied it around his waist. Then he poured water into a basin and began to wash the disciples' feet and to wipe them with the towel that was wrapped around him... (John 13:1-17)

Give to the one who begs from you, and do not refuse the one who would borrow from you. (Matthew 5:42)

Simply doing our duty
He told a story about a servant plowing in the field. Jesus said,

Which of you whose servant comes in from plowing or shepherding in the field will say to him, 'Come at once and sit down to eat'? Instead, won't he tell him, No, he says, 'Prepare my meal, put on your apron, and serve me while I eat. Then you can eat later."

And does the master thank the servant for doing what he was told to do? Of course not. In the same way, when you obey me you should say, 'We are unworthy servants who have simply done our duty.' (Luke 17:7-10)

CHAPTER TEN REFERENCES

How can I repay?
How can I repay the LORD for all His goodness to me? I will lift the cup of salvation and call on the name of the LORD. (Psalm 116:12-13)

Saved out of all our troubles
Many are the afflictions of the righteous: but the LORD delivereth him out of them all. (Psalm 34:19)

The Lord, merciful, gracious, longsuffering
And the Lord passed by before him, and proclaimed, The Lord, The Lord God, merciful and gracious, longsuffering, and abundant in goodness and truth. (Exodus 34:6)

Be of good courage
Wait on the LORD: be of good courage, and he shall strengthen thine heart: wait, I say, on the LORD. (Psalm 27:14)

Peace
Peace I leave with you, my peace I give unto you: not as the world giveth, give I unto you. Let not your heart be troubled, neither let it be afraid. (John 14:27)

Advocate with our Father
My little children, I am writing these things to you so that you will not sin. But if anyone does sin, we have an advocate before the Father— Jesus Christ, the Righteous One. He Himself is the atoning sacrifice for our sins, and not only for ours but also for the sins of the whole world. (1 John 2:1-2)

What does God want?

"And now, O Israel, what does the LORD your God ask of you but to fear the LORD your God by walking in all His ways, to love Him, to serve the LORD your God with all your heart and with all your soul. (Deuteronomy 10:12)

What does God require?

He has shown you, O mankind, what is good. And what does the LORD require of you but to act justly, to love mercy, and to walk humbly with your God? (Micah 6:8)

Freely you have received; freely give

As you go, preach this message: 'The kingdom of heaven is near. Heal the sick, raise the dead, cleanse the lepers, drive out demons. Freely you have received; freely give. (Matthew 10:7-8)

Truly loving means following the rules

And the LORD delivered unto me two tables of stone written with the finger of God; and on them was written according to all the words, which the LORD spake with you in the mount out of the midst of the fire in the day of the assembly. (Deuteronomy 9:10)

God spake all these words… on love

http://www.liveforeverhowto.com/2015/02/06/god-spake-all-these-words/

Keep His commandments

…By this we can be sure that we have come to know Him: if we keep His commandments. If anyone says, "I know Him," but does not keep His commandments, he is a liar, and the truth is not in him. But if anyone keeps

His word, the love of God has been truly perfected in him. By this we know that we are in Him. (1 John 2:4)

Love me and keep my commandments
And shewing mercy unto thousands of them that love me, and keep my commandments. (Exodus 20:6)

And shewing mercy unto thousands of them that love me and keep my commandments. (Deuteronomy 5:10)

If you love me, keep my commandments
If you love me, keep my commandments.(John 14:15)

He that keeps my commandments, is he that loves me
He that hath my commandments, and keeps them, he it is that loves me: and he that loves me shall be loved by my Father, and I will love him, and will manifest myself to him. (John 14:21)

I don't know ye, the lawless ones
But he shall say, I tell you, I don't know who you are; go away, all ye wrongdoers (lawless ones). (Luke 13:27)

Truly loving means following the rules
And the LORD spake unto Moses face to face, as a man speaks to his friend. (Exodus 33:11)

'This commandment that I give you today is certainly not too difficult or not possible for you to keep.' (Deuteronomy 30:11)

Now there was leaning on Jesus' bosom one of His disciples, whom Jesus loved. (John 13:23)

'... His commandments are not hard to keep.' (1 John 5:3)

Become as little children
Jesus said,

Unless you change course, and become as little children, you won't be invited into the kingdom of heaven. (Matthew 18:3)

Wherefore by their fruits shall you recognise them.
By their fruits shall you recognise them.

Not every one that says to me, Lord, Lord, shall enter into the kingdom of heaven; but he that does the will of my Father which is in heaven.

Many will say to me in that day, Lord, Lord, have we not prophesied in your name? and in your name have cast out devils? and in your name done a lot of good?

I will say, I never knew you: go away from me, all you who break God's laws. (Matthew 7:20-23)

For I say unto you, That except your righteousness shall exceed the righteousness of the scribes and Pharisees, ye shall in no case enter into the kingdom of heaven. (Matthew 5:20)

Feed my sheep and follow me
So when they had dined, Jesus saith to Simon Peter, Simon, son of Jonas, lovest thou me more than these? He saith unto him, Yea, Lord; thou knowest that I love thee. He saith unto him, Feed my lambs.

He saith to him again the second time, Simon, son of Jonas, lovest thou me? He saith unto him, Yea, Lord; thou knowest that I love thee. He saith unto him, Feed my sheep.

He saith unto him the third time, Simon, son of Jonas, lovest thou me? Peter was grieved because he said unto him the third time, Lovest thou me? And he said unto him, Lord, thou knowest all things; thou knowest that I love thee. Jesus saith unto him, Feed my sheep. (John 21:15-17)

If you love me, keep my commandments
Showing mercy unto thousands of them that love me, and keep my commandments. (Exodus 20:6)

If ye love me, keep my commandments. (John 14:15)

The whole duty of man
Let us hear the conclusion of the whole matter: Fear God, and keep his commandments: for this is the whole duty of man. (Ecclesiastes 12:13)

CHAPTER ELEVEN REFERENCES

He who does not love does not know God
"Beloved, let us love one another, for love is of God; and everyone who loves is born of God and knows God. He who does not love does not know God, for God is love…We love Him because He first loved us." (I John 4:7-8; 19)

God is love

And we have known and believed the love that God hath to us. God is love; and he that dwelleth in love dwelleth in God, and God in him. (1 John 4:16)

Love each other
We know that we have passed from death unto life, because we love each other. He that doesn't love his brother is already dead. (1 John 3:14)

Mimi says that God made her laugh
https://liveforeverhowto.wordpress.com/god-hath-made-me-to-laugh/

Love God back
Love not the world, neither the things that are in the world. If any man love the world, the love of the Father is not in him. (1 John 2:15)

Passed from death unto life
We know that we have passed from death unto life, because we love each other. He that doesn't love his brother is already dead. (1 John 3:14)

Love your enemies
But I say unto you which hear, Love your enemies, do good to them which hate you,

Bless them that curse you
Bless them that curse you, and pray for them which despitefully use you.

Turn the other cheek
And unto him that smiteth thee on the one cheek offer also the other; and him that taketh away thy cloak forbid not to take thy coat also.

Give to everyone that asks
Give to every man that asketh of thee; and of him that taketh away thy goods ask them not again.

Do unto others
And as ye would that men should do to you, do ye also to them likewise. (Luke 6:27-31)

Quote from Mother Teresa
It's not between you and them, it's between you and your Father in Heaven.

Depart from evil, seek peace, do good
Depart from evil, and do good; seek peace, and pursue it. (Psalm 34:14)

Keep God's commandments and do good
One came and said to Jesus, Good Master, what good thing shall I do, that I may have eternal life?

And Jesus answered, Why call me good? there is no one good but one, that is, God: but if you want to live forever, keep the commandments.

The young man said, Which? Jesus said, Don't murder, Don't commit adultery, Don't steal, Don't bear false witness, Honour your father and thy mother: and, love your neighbour as yourself.

The young man said to Jesus, All these things I've done as long as I can remember: what else?

Jesus answered, If you want to be perfect, go and sell all that you have, and give to the poor, and you shall have treasure in heaven: and come and follow me.

When the young man heard Jesus say that, he went away sad: because he owned lots of stuff.

Then Jesus said to his disciples, Verily I say unto you, It is near impossible for a rich man to get into the kingdom of heaven.

And again I say, It is easier for a camel to go through the eye of a needle than for a rich man to enter into the kingdom of God.

When Jesus' disciples heard this, they were extremely amazed, saying, Who then can be saved?

Jesus said unto them, With men this is impossible; but with God all things are possible. (Matthew 19:16-26)

Love with all your heart
However, loving God with all your heart and with all your understanding and with all your strength, and loving your neighbor as yourself, is way more important than all kinds of offerings and sacrifices." (Mark 12:33)

Let your light shine
Let your light so shine before men, that they may see your good works, and glorify your Father which is in heaven. (Matthew 5:16)

CHAPTER TWELVE REFERENCES

God made me laugh
Sarah said, God hath made me laugh, so that all that hear will laugh with me. (Genesis 21:6)

What is Love? on youtube

197

According to the prophets.

https://youtu.be/hFbBERYN88o

Scripture is by Moses, Jesus, and the Apostle John. Music of this video is courtesy of Art of Noise 'Moments in Love.'

WHAT IS THE LOVE OF GOD?

This is the love of God
This is the love of God, that we keep his commandments: and his commandments are not hard to keep. (1 John 5:3)

This commandment that I give you today is certainly not too difficult or not possible for you to keep. (Deuteronomy 30:11)

This is love
This is love, that we walk according to His commandments. This is the very commandment you have heard from the beginning, that you must walk in love. (2 John 1:6)

Fix my words in your hearts and minds
Fix these words of mine in your hearts and minds, tie them as a sign on your hands and bind them on your foreheads. Teach them to your children. (Deuteronomy 11:18)

My law in their minds and hearts
It will not be like the covenant I made with their fathers when I took them by the hand to lead them out of

Egypt—a covenant they broke, though I was a husband to them," declares the LORD.

"But this is the covenant I will make with the house of Israel after those days, declares the LORD. I will put My law in their minds and inscribe it on their hearts. And I will be their God, and they will be My people.

No longer will each man teach his neighbor or his brother, saying, 'Know the LORD,' because they will all know Me, from the least of them to the greatest, declares the LORD. For I will forgive their iniquity and will remember their sins no more." (Jeremiah 31:32-34)

I delight to do your will
"I delight to do Your will, O my God; Your law is within my heart." (Psalm 40:8)

The Commandments sum up how to love
The law of the Lord is perfect, converting the soul: the testimony of the Lord is sure, making wise the simple.

The statutes of the Lord are right, rejoicing the heart: the commandment of the Lord is pure, enlightening the eyes.

The fear of the Lord is clean, enduring forever: the judgments of the Lord are true and righteous altogether.

More to be desired are they than gold, yea, than much fine gold: sweeter also than honey and the honeycomb.

Moreover by them is thy servant warned: and in keeping of them there is great reward.

Who can understand his errors? cleanse thou me from secret faults.

Keep back thy servant also from presumptuous sins; let them not have dominion over me: then shall I be upright, and I shall be innocent from the great transgression. (Psalm 19:7-13)

Life everlasting
Take to heart all the words which I testify among you this day; command your children to observe to do, all the words of this law.

For it is not a vain thing for you; because it is your life... (Deuteronomy 32:46-47)

For I have not spoken of myself; but the Father which sent me,

he gave me a commandment, what I should say, and what I should speak.

And I know that his commandment is life everlasting:

whatsoever I speak therefore, even as the Father said unto me, so I speak. (John 21:50)

Mary and the alabaster box

You can read about Mary here
https://liveforeverhowto.wordpress.com/2016/03/19/mary-and-the-alabaster-box-2/

You can listen to the song, 'Mary and the Alabaster Box,' here

https://soundcloud.com/peopleisgrass/mary-the-alabaster-box

lyrics from Matthew, Mark, Luke and John

Saved through good work, love and faith
She put the ointment of spikenard, very costly.
She put it on his body for his burial.
Mary wrought a good work on Jesus.
Let her alone.
She done what she could.
Mary wrought a good work on him.
An alabaster box of very precious ointment.
She poured it on his head as he sat at meat.
She done what she could.
She wrought a good work on him.
Mary wrought a good work on Jesus.
Let her alone.
She done what she could.
Spikenard very costly.
With her hair she wiped his feet.
She did it for his burial.
It'll be told for a memorial.

Wondrous things
Open my eyes that I may see the wondrous things from Your law. I am a stranger on the earth; do not hide Your commandments from me. (Psalm 119:18)

Read the whole of Psalm 119.

AFTERWORD REFERENCES

A blessing and a curse
Behold, I set before you this day a blessing and a curse…
(Deuteronomy 11:26-28)

The Commandments a blessing
Behold, I set before you this day a blessing and a curse; A blessing, if ye obey the commandments of the Lord your God, which I command you this day: And a curse, if ye will not obey the commandments of the Lord your God… (Deuteronomy 11:26-28)

Don't listen to Pharisees
'Be careful,' Jesus said. 'Watch out for the yeast of the Pharisees and Sadducees.' (Matthew 16:6)

See also Luke 11:37–54, Matthew 23:1–39, Mark 12:35–40, Luke 20:45–47

Lip service
"…these people draw near to me with their mouths, and honour me with their lips, yet have removed their hearts far from me. Moreover, their worship toward me is the doctrines of men." (Isaiah 29:13)

These people honour Me with their lips, but their hearts are far from Me. They worship Me in vain; they teach as doctrine the precepts of men. (Matthew 15:8)

Be kind, Father
Be kind to your servants Lord, that we may live and obey you. (Psalm 119:17)

God's Commandments

And he gave Moses, when he finished talking with him on mount Sinai, two tables of testimony, tables of stone, written with the finger of God. (Exodus 31:18)

… Listen to all the words and close them in your hearts and command your children to do and keep all the words of this law.

This is not a small thing; it is your life… (Deuteronomy 32:46-47)

I

I am God, who saved you. Only respect and admire me (what is good) and not evil. No other gods.

II

Don't create images or likenesses of anything that is in heaven above, or in the earth beneath, nor of those things that are in the waters under the earth.
Don't admire nor serve them. You and your children and your children's children will be in trouble if you do. I will show mercy unto thousands that love me, and keep my commandments.

III

Don't take my name in vain.

You'll be punished if you do.

IV

Remember to keep one day a week holy; the Sabbath day. You'll work six days but the seventh day is the Sabbath of the Lord thy God. Don't work on that day.

Not you, nor your son, nor your daughter, nor your employee or servant, nor your animals that live with you.
For in six days the Lord made heaven and earth, and the sea, and all things that are in them, and rested on the seventh day: therefore the Lord blessed the seventh day, and sanctified it.

V

Honour your mum and dad;

that you may live long.

VI

Don't kill.

VII

Don't commit adultery.

VIII

Don't steal.

IX

Don't lie.

X

Don't covet.

Eternal life
I know that His commandment leads to eternal life. Therefore I tell you exactly what my Father told me to say. (John 12:50)

This is love

This commandment that I give you today is certainly not too difficult or not possible for you to keep. (Deuteronomy 30:11)

This is the love of God, that we keep his commandments: and his commandments are not hard to keep. (1 John 5:3)

Abundant peace

Abundant peace have they who love Your Law; nothing makes them stumble. (Psalm 119:165)

Other books by Mimi Emmanuel on health, faith & book publishing

are available from Amazon.com & www.mimiemmanuel.com

SHARING FROM HER HEART - "I enjoy Mimi's style of writing. She has a way of drawing the reader in to sit next to her while she wraps her arm around you and tells her tale while you listen." Virginia Ritterbush, #1 Bestselling author of *Reframe Your Viewpoints*

Mimi lives in Wide Bay, Queensland, Australia in a treehouse overlooking the bay with her family, puppies Layla-Joy, Lilac-Delight, and Sweetpea, the rescued magpie.

Lunch is enjoyed with the butcherbirds and geckos, whilst watching the kangaroos with their joeys hop around her front yard.

Mimi was born in Sydney and grew up in Europe. She lived on the beach where she helped her parents in their kiosk. Later on Mimi worked in the medical industry. She burned-out and initiated a career change. Mimi is now living her dream as an author. She writes from her recliner with industrial strength ear mufflers on, and this is how she's become a bestselling author with her books ranking #1 bestsellers in over 40 categories.

Mimi is also a popular inspirational speaker. She can be contacted on her website for speaking engagements and private coaching.

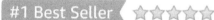

MY STORY OF SURVIVAL
THIS IS A GOD-SEND READ!

"This is a God-send read for those with mysterious food intolerances. Mimi learned how to craft her own survival diet out of just a very few ingredients. She shares her journey to show that there are answers to be found."
#1 Bestselling author of Toolkit for Wellness - Deidre J Edwards

MIMI'S BOOK LAUNCH PLAN
SIMPLY BRILLIANT - A WEALTH OF KNOWLEDGE

"Perfect for all writers… the book is well written - it's like having a trusted friend in the same room with you… Highly recommended."
Bestselling author P Patel

LIVE YOUR BEST LIFE

WOW. THIS BOOK BLEW ME AWAY!

"This is a powerful book. This is the type of book that changes your thinking and can change the world!"

#1 Bestselling author of *Author Your Success* - Ray Brehm

Made in United States
Orlando, FL
18 August 2024

50448825R00117